Guitar

Guitar

The Shape of Sound

100 Iconic Designs

by Ultan Guilfoyle

Design and Technology

The universal desire to make music somehow found three-dimensional form when early humanoids discovered how to get a string to make noise by vibrating it over a semi-enclosed chamber. From that moment more than a thousand years ago, Andrés Segovia, Eddie Van Halen, U2, and the guitar solo were all but inevitable.

The prehistory of guitar design takes a single-string instrument from West Africa and through a series of evolutionary leaps and some spectacular carpentry arrives at the oud of North Africa and the Middle East. The bowl-back, fretless oud, with a short neck and a big body, can still be heard played with brilliance all over the Middle East. Migrating north, the oud became, in French, *l'oud*. From there it was a short linguistic hop to the lute, in Italian, *liuto*.

Taking the oud and the lute as the great-grandparents of the guitar, we find ourselves in medieval Europe, where the guitar slowly evolved—through a variety of shapes, sizes, and numbers of strings—into the guitar we recognize today. The vihuela, a miracle of Spanish instrument-making abilities, had six pairs of double strings, called "courses," and a body of music written for it. Spain in the seventeenth century had a big influence on the evolution of the baroque guitar, and in Venice, the German Sellas brothers—Giorgio and Matteo—made gut-stringed, five-course baroque guitars in the style of the Spanish *chitarra spagnola*. Guitarists playing the Sellas brothers' instruments catered to the Venetians' love of songs and airs, many of which were published using an early form of guitar notation, the *alfabeto*.

The seventeenth-century Italian playing style evolved further, and with it came a new design, the *chitarra battente*—a loud steel-string guitar made for strumming that was largely for folk musicians. Serious music aficionados wanted to play music by the great masters, including Monteverdi and Vivaldi. Luthiers, including the Sellas brothers, took advantage of this growing interest in serious music and made guitars of great quality and beauty, with ornamentation that included a new mustache motif on the bridge. This hairy design detail would continue well into the twentieth century, even appearing in abstract form on the bridge of Gibson acoustics, including the SJ-100 and SJ-200 jumbo guitars.

By the late seventeenth century, Antonio Stradivari—from his workshop in Cremona, Italy, some 140 miles (225 km) southwest of Venice—had established the greatest luthier workshop of the age, one that produced instruments that are treasured and still played today. Those instruments are, of course, Stradivari's violins. Less well-known are Stradivari's guitars, of which only two survive in their original condition.

Stradivari was such a giant that his design of the guitar would remain the standard form for almost a century, until well into the 1800s.

In Spain in the early 1800s, the Pagés brothers in Cádiz brought guitar design completely into the modern era, and although they were still using double strings, or "courses," rather than the single-string arrangements of the modern era, the shape and structure of their instruments are recognizable as the classical guitar we know today. Elsewhere, in both France and Italy, instead of an arrangement of double strings, six single strings were becoming standard due to their simplicity and ease of tuning. The use of six single strings also reduced the stresses on the guitar's structure created by six courses of double strings. René Lacôte was the great Parisian maker of the early 1800s. The guitars he produced were advanced; however, they still featured some design motifs of old, principally the mustachioed bridge.

In Vienna the guitars being made by luthier Johann Stauffer—who had a young and brilliant C. F. Martin as his workshop foreman—still had the mustache bridge but showed significant advances, especially in the headstock. Looking forward to something Leo Fender and Freddie Tavares might have cooked up more than a century later with the Telecaster and Stratocaster headstocks, Stauffer created an extravagant headstock design that was a huge leap forward in the tunability of guitars. With all six tuners aligned on one side, the player could tune the guitar more easily, and the strings could run in six parallel lines from the head to the bridge of the guitar.

Martin, of course, took this design with him when he set up his own guitar-making business, first in New York City and shortly thereafter in Nazareth, Pennsylvania (where it remains to this day). Martin eventually abandoned the Stauffer headstock for more traditional Spanish-style

A fashionably well-dressed lady plays her lute in this painting by Andrea Solario, 1520.

The ornate mustache bridge is a feature of this seventeenth-century Italian *chitarra battente*.

Headstock designs. Clockwise from top left,
Stradivari, 1688; Stauffer, 1840; Fender, 1961,
and Danelectro, 1959.

Design and Technology

tuners. Martin also revised another old-world concept by creating an X-brace for his guitar tops, eschewing the fan bracing so beloved by European luthiers. The bracing in an acoustic guitar's top is to prevent the thin top—usually made of spruce—from flexing and warping both when it is played and, more important, as the wood adapts to changing environments and relative humidity.

In Spain in the 1850s, Antonio de Torres Jurado established the style and build of classical Spanish guitars that would remain the standard for 150 years. Most notably, Torres enlarged the guitar's body by almost a quarter; established a new, longer string length; used mechanical tuners; and used a saddle on the bridge. All of these innovations created a truly professional-quality instrument that was suited to public performances in larger venues. The greatest, most widely traveled virtuoso of the day was Francisco Tárrega, and he played, naturally, a Torres guitar.

The immigration boom of the nineteenth century and the mobility of huge numbers of new immigrants across the United States, especially to the great urban centers of the Midwest—Chicago, Detroit, Cincinnati, and St. Louis—brought a huge demand for musical instruments of all forms. The steel strings of bigger guitars made them louder than the gut-stringed form of the classical guitar, and these instruments became the standard-bearer for Martin and its many competitors, including Washburn and a new upstart, Gibson.

The word *genius* is, these days, bandied about in such a carefree way that it is easy to forget that some people really *are* geniuses—thinkers who create and develop new ideas that in some way change our world. Or at least their world. One such genius was Orville H. Gibson, founder of the eponymous Gibson Mandolin-Guitar

Manufacturing Co., Ltd. of Kalamazoo, Michigan, which was established in 1902. For almost ten years before he started making guitars, Orville Gibson made beautiful mandolins and violins. He was familiar with traditional methods of lutherie, which included how to make carved wooden instruments, such as violins and cellos. A carved top, as on a cello, is inherently rigid and needs very little bracing to be stiff enough to resist the warping and flexing that bedevils a flattop instrument. Gibson took the idea of the carved top of a cello and applied it to the top, sides, and back of a guitar. The result was the Gibson Style O (for the oval sound hole) guitar, the first carved-top guitar. Except Gibson called his guitar an archtop.

Although Orville Gibson apparently experienced a mental health issue and was sidelined by his colleagues at Gibson for being "eccentric," his great innovations were picked up enthusiastically by his colleagues, and Gibson went on to become the foremost guitar maker in the world. Archtop guitars, which were at first purely acoustic, eventually became electric with the invention of the pickup. They dominated the world of jazz, and they remain in production today.

By the early 1900s, the explosion in folk music that accompanied the wave of immigration led to a demand for bigger, louder guitars; musicians wanted instruments that could hold their own in public, where the crowds were not only getting bigger, they were getting rowdier, too. In response to this public demand, Martin's luthiers began to make their guitars bigger. The HMS *Dreadnought*, launched in 1906, was the prize of the British Royal Navy; it was the biggest, baddest battleship ever made. Martin decided to borrow the name for its new giant guitar. Martin Dreadnoughts have been in production since 1916, but initially Martin didn't want to risk putting its name on the big guitar. Instead, Martin allowed the music publishing giant Oliver Ditson to bundle the guitar with its popular sheet music. The big, macho guitar was a huge hit and Martin quickly put its name on the headstock. Martin Dreadnoughts have been the gold standard of American acoustic guitars ever since.

The cutaway on the lower body of a guitar, formed to let the player reach the higher frets, first appeared on the Gibson Style O, designed by Gibson's George Laurian, in 1903. It seems like a modest design gesture, but it had Italian antecedents and has been used by many luthiers since. To distinguish between a soft, round cutaway and a hard-edged, sharp cutaway, the terms *Venetian* and *Florentine* have become standard; the former for the soft profile, the latter for the hard-edged profile. Whether these names were adopted because they fit the characteristics of the people of those cities is not known.

By 1920, Gibson's Lloyd Loar had taken over guitar design from Orville Gibson, and again the word genius seems apt for Loar's innovations. The Gibson L-5 of 1922 was Loar's response to the need for a larger, louder guitar. An archtop with elegant f-holes instead of a sound hole, and with a beautiful tone to go with its classical looks, the L-5 lent itself readily to folk music and jazz, especially when played by early country guitarist Maybelle Carter or jazz great Eddie Lang.

Although the archtop is a particularly American idea, it was taken up with fantastic skill and invention by two of the most interesting luthiers of the twentieth century, whose own guitar-making preferences owed more to nineteenth-century Italy and the great tradition of Italian violin makers—including Stradivari, Guarneri, and Amati—than to anything cooked up in the American Midwest. Perhaps because New York City had a huge Italian immigrant population, or perhaps because it was a great jazz city, John D'Angelico focused on the archtop guitar for a personal application of his lutherie. Rich in Art Deco detailing, D'Angelico's guitars were custom-made for the very best musicians of the time. On D'Angelico's death in 1964, Jimmy D'Aquisto—once D'Angelico's apprentice and protégé—picked up the form and took it to even greater artistic and technical heights, at once modern and modernist. Immediately his guitars became both highly prized and highly priced.

Today, John Monteleone has taken the Italian-American archtop concept to unimagined heights of artistry, expressiveness, and technical brilliance. Monteleone's guitars are played by the greatest players and are installed in New York's Metropolitan Museum of Art. Monteleone has also become a mentor to a new generation of archtop luthiers, including Bryant Trenier, who, although based in France, is himself American.

The virtuoso classical guitarist Andrés Segovia was born in the Andalusian city of Linares, Spain, just before the turn of the twentieth century. Segovia was, therefore, perfectly positioned—both in time and place—to take advantage of the popularity of Spanish classical music in the first half of the twentieth century; he was a brilliant musician who came to dominate classical guitar music. Segovia was devoted to his José Ramírez guitar, which he believed to be as great a guitar as was possible to make. Segovia inspired Hermann Hauser in Munich to take his German tradition of guitar making—very much in line with what Johann Stauffer had been doing in Vienna a century earlier—to an even higher level with his own version of the Spanish guitar design. Hauser dissected Spanish guitars, including those of Torres and Ramírez, and not only extended the refinements of their fan bracing but paid particular attention to the guitar's spruce top, creating a thicker top that had a slight bow. Segovia described his 1937 Hauser to be the "greatest guitar of our epoch." In 1986, shortly before his death, Segovia's wife gifted the guitar to the Metropolitan Museum of Art in New York, where it remains.

Perhaps the stagnation of the classical guitar itself has to do with the decline of classical guitar music, which was until recently relegated to the repertoire of baroque Italy, Germany, and Spain. The great innovations of Torres, Ramírez, and Hauser remained in place until the end of the twentieth century, when luthiers again looked at the classical guitar for ways forward, both in aesthetics and in technology. A chance conversation between classical guitarist John Williams and luthier Greg Smallman, both from Australia, about the "perfection" of Williams's guitar—made by Ignacio Fleta—led to Smallman making advances in classical guitar design. These improvements were manifested in the top, where Smallman created an ultrathin table, braced by a honeycomb of Nomex, and in the fingerboards, which he began making of carbon fiber. Smallman is not, of course, the only innovator. Gifted guitar makers from around the world are making significant guitars, including Jim Redgate, another celebrated luthier from Australia.

In the 1970s Bill Collings represented a new generation of luthiers determined to break into the world of high-end acoustic guitars. When discussing guitars with up-and-coming country singer/songwriter Lyle Lovett in Dallas, in about 1978, Collings said, "Well, you have your Martins and you have your Gibsons, and that's it." Collings's design philosophy was simply to take the sizes and styles of the best Martin and Gibson acoustic guitars and to make them much better. Collings was obsessed with making a guitar with tones that were even across all six strings, something that was notoriously absent from even the best Martin guitars at the time. Collings was not alone. Also in the mid-1970s, a young Bob Taylor began making his own guitars in San Diego, California, experimenting with new neck designs and acoustic guitar electronics, as well as exploring different, smaller guitar shapes. At the same time, Canadian luthier Jean Larrivée made his mark with a series of different-sized guitars,

including a parlor guitar, which redefined the very idea of a small guitar made to the highest quality. All three guitar makers have become significant leaders in the design and manufacture of modern acoustic guitars and, along with others—including Stuart Mossman, James Olson, and, in Ireland, George Lowden—have brought the design and build of acoustic guitars to hitherto undreamed-of standards.

Luthier, educator, and musician Dana Bourgeois designs and builds acoustic guitars from his Maine workshop that have become the gold standard for virtuoso bluegrass players. Bourgeois has also led a contemporary trend away from the bigger, Dreadnought-sized acoustic guitars toward smaller, more easily playable, more sonically pure guitars.

In 1992 electronics wizard and guitar maker Leo Fender was inducted into the Rock and Roll Hall of Fame. The man chosen to induct Fender was Rolling Stones guitarist Keith Richards. In his remarks, Richards said that while Leo did, indeed, create the Telecaster and the Stratocaster, he did something even greater: "he invented the amplifier." Richards's glowing attribution was not true, of course, because guitar amps had been invented decades earlier than Leo's first combo amp, but his point was well made. In the middle of the twentieth century, the use of electronics to pick up and amplify the sounds from a guitar's strings changed the world forever.

Vaudeville showman George Beauchamp's fingerprints are all over the history of guitar making and amplification. Having started the National company with the Dopyera brothers, John and Rudy, to build and sell "resophonic" guitars—which were, in effect, self-amplifying acoustic guitars—in 1931 Beauchamp went a step further. With partners Paul Barth and Swiss immigrant Adolph Rickenbacker, Beauchamp formed the Ro-Pat-In Corporation and presented

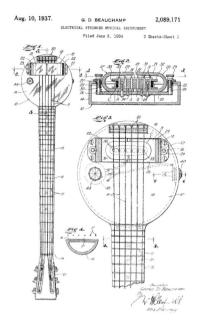

the world with an amplified lap steel Hawaiian guitar, the Rickenbacker Frying Pan. Although the Stromberg-Voisinet company in Chicago had designed an amplified guitar a few years earlier, it never went into production, and the Rickenbacker Frying Pan was to become definitively the first electric guitar. Beauchamp's early Rickenbacker guitars, including a more commonly styled Electro Spanish (also made in 1931), were not easy to play and were notoriously prone to noisy feedback. However, they sent a huge signal to guitar makers everywhere: amplification was here, and it was going to change everything.

Gibson was quick to respond and invented pickups for several of its guitars before settling on a single-coil blade-type pickup in the neck position for their ES-150 (the *ES* standing for *Electric Spanish*). Benny Goodman's guitarist Charlie Christian took up the ES-150 and made it his own, to the point that the guitar's "blade" pickup came to be known as the Charlie Christian pickup.

The floodgates were now open. Immediately after World War II, Leo Fender, who had a well-known radio store in Fullerton, south of Los Angeles, brought his knowledge of electronics to bear on the sound of the guitar. With the help of friend and custom guitar maker and engineer Paul Bigsby, Leo Fender and his crew—most notably guitarist Freddie Tavares—went to work on a playable solid-body guitar with two pickups and an amplifier to match. The result was the Broadcaster, soon to be renamed the Telecaster. And this was followed quickly by the three-pickup Stratocaster. These two Fender guitars, along with Gibson's Les Paul, would dominate the shapes and the very sounds of electric guitars for the next half century. East-coast based Les Paul, whose early work on a playable electric guitar had echoed the work done by Beauchamp, Rickenbacker, and Fender on the West Coast, was not only a design genius; he was the most popular guitar player in the United States. His

Rickenbacker Frying Pan patent, 1937.

Testing the electronics of a Telecaster in the Fullerton, California, Fender factory, c.1950.

liaison with Gibson would prove hugely profitable for both. Gibson Les Pauls were expensive guitars, beautifully made in Michigan. While they sold in huge numbers for their target demographic, the Fenders sold equally well at the less expensive end of the working guitarist's market.

The shapes of those early electric guitars, particularly the Stratocaster, which had been sketched out by Tavares in the Fender workshop, came to define the look of an electric guitar. Rickenbacker, through the work of German designer Roger Rossmeisl, went a different way, with unique shapes that, although more exotic (and expensive) than the Fenders, also found great success. Rossmeisl's use of slight, imaginative design details, including a glorious, filleted indent carved around the edge of the body, known as the "German carve," set a design standard for the electric guitar. All of these guitars from Fender, Gibson, and Rickenbacker are still in production, a testament to the timelessness of great design.

Despite a flood of beautifully shaped and made guitars from elsewhere in the United States, Great Britain, and Japan, guitarists have been notoriously reluctant to deviate from the paradigmatic shapes of Fenders and Gibsons. Until relatively recently, that is, due to an entirely new movement in modern guitar design driven by the Internet and by advances in computer-controlled design and manufacture, including 3D printing. The younger generation of luthier-designers were born to parents who themselves were not yet born in the era of Leo Fender and Les Paul. And their designs have burst out in new and exciting directions. Guitarist and designer Tosin Abasi, whose beautiful fan-fret seven-string electric guitars are suited to his own style of highly dexterous metal playing, shows that guitarists can make their own guitars and ones that are every bit as good as anything from Fender and Gibson. Artist-craftsmen, including Nicolai Schorr in Berlin, Florian Bouyou in

Montreal, and Michael King in St. Louis, Missouri, are all redefining the shapes and sounds of contemporary electric guitars.

In guitar making, as in every field of endeavor, there are outliers who demand attention, not least because they go in altogether surprising and different directions. Two of those outlying luthiers are women. Linda Manzer in Toronto and French luthier Rachel Rosenkrantz, working in Rhode Island, make guitars of unusual shapes and materials with unique voices that simply demand to be heard.

The future of guitar design looks bright, with modern luthiers applying computer design and milling techniques to the art of guitar building. The shape of the Stratocaster as the paradigm of guitar design has also been brushed aside, not only by guitar makers but by the players, who demand better playability and more forward-looking shapes for their instruments.

Music

"All I've got is a red guitar, three chords, and the truth." — Harlan Howard, Country Singer/Songwriter

The first guitar in our timeline, the so-called Hill guitar, was made by Antonio Stradivari in 1688, when the three great masters of the Baroque— Johann Sebastian Bach, George Frederic Handel, and Antonio Vivaldi—were at the peak of their considerable creative output. Yet, while we can listen to great violin music from these masters, played on violins by Stradivari and his contemporaries, we don't have an equivalently large body of music written for Stradivari's guitars. What we assume, therefore, is that music for the guitar, while widely popular, was music for private performance in the home and not for public performance by virtuoso professionals.

From the marvelous skills that Stradivari brought to his guitars, and his groundbreaking form making, the guitar was clearly not a second-class citizen. Instead, it was an expensive, often extravagantly ornamented, perfectly made instrument on a par with a cello or violin. But it was made for domestic use, for music of the chamber, perhaps played by young ladies, as was so often portrayed in the art of the time. The guitar was not for playing great sonatas, nor was it for accompanying orchestras in the playing of concertos, such as Bach's violin concertos or Vivaldi's *Four Seasons*, which are still among the most popular violin works today.

Niccolò Paganini, who was born in 1782, a mere forty years after Vivaldi's death, was the greatest violinist of his era and his music for the violin represents some of the greatest, and most technically difficult, of all string writing. Paganini was a virtuoso who only played the greatest instruments of his time, including a Giuseppe Guarneri and a notable Stradivari. It turns out that Paganini played the guitar, and he played it very well. Paganini also wrote for the guitar, notably some wonderful trios for violin, guitar, and cello. Paganini owned important guitars made by the best Parisian makers, including Alexandre Voboam. And he brought one everywhere on his many travels, playing it constantly. But his attitude toward the guitar suggests that it was an instrument for private performance. He never played his guitar in public, regarding it as a private instrument, a true "chamber" guitar. The guitar may have been considered a lesser instrument in the eyes of the cognoscenti; whatever the reason, Paganini—the greatest musician of his time—kept his guitar playing to himself and his close musician friends. Paganini the guitarist lived, it seems, in a velvet-lined closet.

As an instrument, the guitar was in high demand, whether made in Italy by Stradivari or in Germany by master craftsmen such as Joachim Tielke, whose extraordinarily ornamented instruments told of wealthy connoisseur clients. Guitars of the highest quality were made all over Europe and were widely played and enjoyed. Some music was being written by guitarists for guitarists.

Mauro Giuliani, for example, an Italian virtuoso and an acquaintance of Paganini, was writing serious music and performing widely in Europe. And Paganini himself wrote music with his friend and occasional collaborator Luigi Legnani.

The Spanish style of classical guitar came to us from the high Baroque of the 1600s, and is with us still, virtually unchanged for three hundred years. Louis Panormo, a nineteenth-century London luthier, advertised himself to be the "only maker of guitars in the Spanish style," and here is a clue to the music being played on Panormo's guitars. A century after Bach and Vivaldi, the predominant music for the guitar was coming from Spain, from composer/players such as Fernando Sor, who greatly influenced his compatriot Francisco Tárrega. Tárrega was one of those guitarists who, in spite of the guitar's limitations as an instrument for public performance, built a career as a famous performer. A true virtuoso, Tárrega had a demanding concert schedule, from Madrid and Barcelona to Paris and London. Indeed, it was on a trip to London that Tárrega—cold, lonely, and miserable—composed what is today his most popular work, "Lágrima," which means "a tear." This little tune has been recorded many times, and by some of the greatest players, including Andrés Segovia, Narciso Yepes, and Julian Bream.

While Spanish music became the standard repertoire for the concert guitar, at least into the mid- to late twentieth century, a small moment in Germany would provide the impetus for some of the most important guitar music. The great Viennese guitar maker Johann Georg Stauffer employed a young German cabinetmaker, C. F. Martin, first as an apprentice and later as his workshop foreman. Martin's own family had a well-known cabinetmaking business in Germany. Martin returned to take over the family business in about 1820, after his employment with Stauffer, but he ran afoul of the local guild of violin makers. The guild, in a series of complaints during the

Engraving showing Antonio Stradivari in his workshop.

Francisco Tárrega playing one of his Torres guitars.

1820s in which Martin was named, sought to prevent mere "cabinetmakers" from making violins and other stringed instruments. Aggrieved by the constraints placed on his work by the violin makers, Martin emigrated to New York, where in 1833 he set up a small store on Hudson Street in lower Manhattan.

Martin's arrival in New York coincided with a huge wave of immigration from all over Europe, which would continue for another century and a half. And these new immigrants brought with them the songs and folk tunes of their homelands. Soon a diasporic boom in traditional and ethnic music was under way with the accompaniment of banjos, accordions, fiddles and, of course, guitars. Immigrants from Ireland and Scotland, bringing with them their rich tradition of complex and difficult Celtic airs and tunes, drove this new boom in folk music. Along with the old ballad and troubadour songs that were imported by English immigrants, this new American folk music, with heady injections of French folk tunes (the French-Canadian former colony of Acadie gave rise to the term *Cajun*) and German polkas, had a polyglot momentum that was impossible to resist.

Martin's early guitars were small, parlor-size guitars, typical of European guitars. But this land of opportunity, this New World, was a garrulous, noisy place. The people were noisy, the towns and cities were noisy, and the nightlife was very noisy. Nineteenth-century American troubadours needed to be heard above the polyphony, and Martin was happy to accommodate the demand for bigger, louder guitars.

Country music and bluegrass emerged from this heady mix of Irish, Scottish, and English folk music. Growing in appeal from the end of the nineteenth century until the 1950s, bluegrass became the beneficiary of the musical demands of the complex melodic filigrees of Celtic jigs, reels, and hornpipes. It took two virtuoso players

to bring the guitar fully into focus as a solo bluegrass instrument. Clarence White would go on to greater fame as a member of the Byrds in the early 1960s, but it was as a bluegrass player that he took the guitar to the front of the stage, soloing freely in a way that had not been done before. Inspired by Clarence White, Tony Rice took virtuoso playing to an even higher level and changed the bluegrass sound forever. Clarence White's influence on Tony Rice was so profound that the latter tracked down White's famous Martin, bought the guitar, and played it for the rest of his own career. From there, a host of great guitarists have taken bluegrass from hillbilly music to the forefront of musical culture, with bands such as Union Station and Nickel Creek, led by musicians as great as Jeff White, Chris Thile, Alison Krauss, Dan Tyminski, and Jerry Douglas, among many others.

As popular as country music and bluegrass became in the twentieth century, another distinctive genre, made for the guitar and played on the guitar, evolved in parallel: the blues. The emergence of the blues was significant not just for guitar music. The blues, simply, is the most important musical and pop cultural genre to emerge in one hundred-and-fifty years.

"It's easy to play the blues. It's just hard to feel the blues." — Jimi Hendrix

Jimi Hendrix's throwaway comment about the blues is, on its face, a flip aphorism and not a nugget of philosophical truth from a great musician. Dismissing these words, however, would be to deny the roots of the blues, and the generations of men and women who sang and played the blues. This great body of music was of a people displaced by the violence of kidnapping, the horror of slavery and torture, and the daily unspeakable fear of unknowable violence and death. The simple, happy village tunes of West Africa—songs of birds in the air, of crops in the fields, of young love in spring—were transmuted by slavery into the dirges of deep, existential pain. They were the songs of the blues. That is why Jimi Hendrix was right.

The blues were forged in history but evolved into a musical form that became the engine of popular music as we now hear and understand it. For guitar players, it was deceptively simple—the twelve-bar, three-chord structure around which simple, plaintive narratives could be built, then played and sung, then handed on to the next. The greatest blues guitarists—among them Son House, Robert Johnson, Charlie Patton, Rosetta Tharpe, Muddy Waters, and Howlin' Wolf—all felt that existential pain of a people still not free, still subjected to the deep injustices of daily racism, but still singing, hollering, crying, and playing their histories. Where would we be without them? Without these players, we wouldn't know the rushing guitar rhythms of funk. We wouldn't thrill to R&B. We wouldn't have Nile Rodgers or Prince or the Beatles or the Rolling Stones. Of if we did, they would sound very different.

The early twentieth century saw greater movement of people than ever before, with greater stability, an emerging middle class, and greater access to all types of entertainment. As soon as movies could be heard—ironically starting with the all-important *The Jazz Singer* in 1927—music as a recorded form took off. At the same time, broadcasting over the airwaves, and the availability of inexpensive radio receivers, put this new technology in virtually every home. Music was now fully democratized, seen, listened to, and emulated by millions of people. The age of the musical, whether in theaters or on the big screen, had arrived, and with it came a canon of American music that has come to be known as the Great American Songbook.

Big bands took this music to theaters all over Europe and the United States, but the music these

Big Bill Broonzy playing his beautiful Style O in 1925.

Sister Rosetta Tharpe, c.1959, playing her 1953 Gibson Les Paul. Note the tailpiece.

Muddy Waters with his Telecaster, 1964.

bands played was almost always American. The bands themselves were based around brass and wind ensembles, supported by a piano, a singer, a double bass, and a guitarist playing a rhythm part. This music was loud, brash, and swinging. The guitars of this era were almost always the acoustic archtops that we have come to know well, especially the Gibsons, which dominated, but also the Epiphones and the glorious early Gretsch archtops. The big band era would develop a separate strain of smaller ensembles often featuring the guitar as both a rhythm and solo instrument, but they all had the same imperative: more volume. It was not possible to make a guitar much bigger than the biggest Gibson of the day, and just as technology had brought sound to movies, it brought amplification to the guitar. The greatest guitarist of this era, Charlie Christian brought big band swing music into the mainstream with his brilliant solo playing for various Benny Goodman ensembles, with Goodman being one of the most famous performers of the time.

In Europe in the 1920s, especially in France, a hybrid jazz form emerged, driven both by American-style swing and a quirky gypsy musical form that soon influenced French popular music in a profound way. Josephine Baker—Black, brilliant, and beloved by the French for her very outsiderness—was a superstar in France and was hugely influential on the development of French jazz. France's own unique gypsy jazz thrived alongside Baker's smoky nightclub swing. Gypsy guitarist Django Reinhardt teamed up with fiddler Stéphane Grappelli to form the Quintette du Hot Club de France, one of the great string ensembles of all time. Django Reinhardt's solo playing was unlike anything heard in the United States. He played on an acoustic guitar, the Selmer Maccaferri, which has come to define the sound of French jazz guitar to this day.

Two American jazz players stand out for bringing the guitar to the front of the stage:

Wes Montgomery and Joe Pass. Montgomery spent his youth learning Charlie Christian solos on his guitar. A welder by day and a musician by night, Montgomery honed a self-taught brilliance that took some time to emerge. It first did so when, at the age of twenty-five, he was employed by bandleader Lionel Hampton, who had heard Montgomery play while touring Indianapolis and immediately offered him a job. Seizing that first opportunity, Wes Montgomery built a career as a performer and a major recording artist. By the time of his untimely death in 1968, at the age of forty-eight, Montgomery had come to define modern jazz guitar playing. The sound of his playing, the lines, the chord progressions, the harmonics, and the octaves became the dominant style of Jazz guitar virtually until the end of the century. Montgomery's picking style was soft and smooth, largely because he picked with the fleshy part of this thumb and not with a pick. His music, with smooth legato and a flowing line, was widely influential on virtually everyone who followed, from George Benson to Pat Metheny.

Joe Pass began performing as a young teen in the mid-1940s and started traveling with small jazz acts. He eventually moved to New York City, where he was exposed to the world of drugs. This life quickly caught up with him, and he spent much of the 1950s in and out of prison and battling an addiction to heroin, among other things. Once Pass overcame his many addictions, his guitar virtuosity, bordering on genius, came into full bloom. Perhaps not as influential as Montgomery, nevertheless, Pass made a profound mark on modern jazz as part of one of the great jazz trios with Oscar Peterson, as an unaccompanied solo player, and by accompanying Ella Fitzgerald on six of her greatest recordings.

In contemporary jazz playing, Pat Metheny stands above all the others, including exceptional guitarists Jim Hall, Allan Holdsworth, John

Scofield, Bill Frisell, Barney Kessel, and contemporary player Mary Halvorson. Metheny changed the trajectory of music for the guitar away from the show tunes that, for almost a century, came to be accepted as jazz "standards." Metheny's line, his unique improvising of a melody, often on the high E string, is both musically complex and heartachingly beautiful. He has a singer's expressiveness, a virtuoso technique, and an instinct for harmonics and chord voicings that have taken the form of contemporary jazz guitar in a direction unimagined by the twentieth-century greats. Whether he is playing a slow ballad or a fusion-style rocker, Metheny's musicianship and love of melody are always close to the surface. It is no accident that Joni Mitchell chose Pat Metheny for the tour that followed her jazz album, *Mingus*, which itself spawned the brilliant live record *Shadows and Light*. It was this album that began a new understanding of Joni Mitchell's own guitar playing, full of sophisticated, open-chord voicings and rhythms, which is only now being fully recognized for its own unique position in the world of popular guitar music.

Metheny's earliest guitar was an archtop, the Gibson ES-175, and the archtop guitar is, almost without exception, the guitar of choice for jazz players. At its greatest, in the case of D'Angelico or D'Aquisto, the archtop rivals the greatest instruments of all time. Among contemporary luthiers of the archtop guitar, John Monteleone stands out, not only for the stunning beauty of his instruments but for his contribution to the canon of commissioned jazz music. As a lover of Italian music of the Baroque era, and Antonio Vivaldi in particular, in 2011 Monteleone set out to commission a guitar quartet in homage to Vivaldi's *Four Seasons* violin concertos. Monteleone chose jazz guitar virtuoso and composer Anthony Wilson to compose the quartet, called *Seasons*, and Monteleone, for his part, created four guitars

In this photograph by Robert Altman, Joni Mitchell cradles her Martin D-28 while Graham Nash whispers into her ear at the 1969 Big Sur Folk Festival.

John Williams and Julian Bream, pictured together here in 1972, transformed classical guitar playing and repertoire in the late twentieth century.

specifically to be played for the piece. These four guitars—called, of course, the Four Seasons—are now in the permanent collection of the Metropolitan Museum of Art in New York City. Wilson's quartet is a stunning blend of closely orchestrated themes and free-form improvisations, demanding virtuoso playing from all four guitarists. It is not only one of the most important additions to contemporary music but also one of the great pieces of writing for the guitar, and it cements Wilson's reputation as a guitarist/composer.

Monteleone's gesture in commissioning such a major piece for a guitar ensemble may eventually be seen as a watershed moment in classical guitar repertoire. Stuck in the Bach transcriptions played by Segovia, and in spite of the efforts of towering musicians such as Julian Bream and his Australian contemporary, John Williams, classical music for the guitar has remained in a blind alley for almost a century. Today, the classical repertoire is bifurcated, with half of the repertoire looking back to Segovia, while the other half, often with a Fender Stratocaster in hand, looks elsewhere for inspiration and something to play. Works such as Wilson's *Seasons*, and a new generation of classical guitarist/composers—of which James Moore, a young electric guitarist from New York, is at the fore—is where the future of classical guitar surely lies. Moore was commissioned by the Chicago Symphony Orchestra to translate his *Sleep Is Shattered* piece for electric guitar into a showpiece for a chamber orchestra, and it received its concert premiere in 2022.

The archtop guitar has had a limited role to play in rock and pop music, with some exceptions. One of the most famous guitars in the history of popular music is John Lennon's Epiphone Casino, a guitar that is featured heavily in Peter Jackson's 2021 movie *The Beatles: Get Back*. The Beatles' role in the evolution of popular music cannot be overstated, nor can their status as the first true guitar band. The Epiphone Casino was something of a band guitar, first used by Paul McCartney, with George Harrison and John Lennon quickly following suit. However, Lennon was the one who, more than the others, came to treasure the Epiphone's light weight, its playability, and its rich sound. Lennon considered himself to be a rhythm guitarist, saying in a *Rolling Stone* interview that he was the "forgotten" guitarist in the Beatles. As if. In that same interview, he said that he "drove" the band, giving the songs their rhythmic pulse. But Lennon could play beautiful, fragmentary solos, such as on "Get Back."

Although McCartney was famously the bass player of the Beatles, he had, in fact, started as a guitarist. When it came time to replace Stuart Sutcliffe, the original bass player, McCartney wryly puts it that neither Lennon nor Harrison would even consider taking on the role. So it fell to him. From that moment on, he changed both the sound and the place of the bass guitar in popular music.

Harrison was a guitar fanatic, recognized almost instantly by McCartney when they first became school friends. Harrison's guitar playing in the Beatles deserves a book of its own, but if one song were to exemplify his brilliance, it would be one of his two most famous, and one of the Beatles' very best: "Something." This is guitar playing at its finest—for the way he bends, and doesn't; for his choices in the melody line; and for his chord transitions both out of, and into, the song.

A second Harrison song demands discussion as well: "While My Guitar Gently Weeps." We know so much about the song, and have heard so many covers, that half a century later, the only mystery is why he gave the solo part to his great friend Eric Clapton and did not play it himself. Had George Harrison written and played his own solo, the world might well have been a different place. Clapton's solo playing is characteristically inventive and brilliant, with a sure line and perfect phrasing. This recording neatly concludes Clapton's early era as a guitarist with the Yardbirds, John Mayall & the Bluesbreakers, Cream, Blind Faith, and Derek and the Dominoes. Clapton often seemed to rise to the challenge of playing with the preeminent players. This was the case with the Beatles, and again with Greg Allman, when they recorded the 1970 album, *Layla and Other Assorted Love Songs*. As good as Clapton was with those bands, little of his subsequent work compares to his legato playing on George Harrison's timeless paean to love and the guitar.

The date 9 February 1964 was a pivotal one in popular guitar music, and both Harrison and Lennon were again at the heart of the story. It was the day of the Beatles' famous *Ed Sullivan Show* television appearance, their first in the United States. Thanks to a letter from the owner of the Rose Morris store in London, the owner of Rickenbacker, F. C. Hall, arranged to meet Lennon, Harrison, and Beatles manager Brian Epstein in a hotel in New York City to show them some new guitars. George was feeling a little under the weather and stayed in bed. Lennon and Epstein met Hall at his hotel, and Lennon tried the guitars. He asked if they could go back to show the guitars to George, so they got in a cab and went back. George loved the new twelve-string, and John chose the six-string. Six months later, in August 1964, the Beatles movie *A Hard Day's Night* was released. Roger McGuinn and his bandmates in the Byrds, looking for a sound that would break them out of folk music and into something bigger, went to a screening of the movie and made notes of all the instruments the Beatles played, including Ringo's drum kit. McGuinn loved the sound of Harrison's Rickenbacker 360/12 and immediately bought one. A year later, the Byrds released *Mr. Tambourine Man*, their debut album, with lovely close harmonies in the singing that owed as much to the Beatles as it

Hank Marvin plays his Guyatone with Cliff Richard, 1959.

George Harrison strumming his Rickenbacker 360/12 during the filming of *A Hard Day's Night* in 1964.

did to their neighbors, the Beach Boys. Most important, the record featured the unmistakable jangly guitar sound of the Rickenbacker twelve-string. The album and the hit single of the same name catapulted the Byrds to international fame, all due to McGuinn's playing of the guitar that Harrison played in *A Hard Day's Night*. The sound of the American guitar band was born, and the music world flipped on its axis once more.

If one musician can be said to have created a bridge between the blues and rock music, and to have forged an entirely new direction for guitar-driven rock music, it is Jimi Hendrix. Deeply intelligent, hugely gifted, and with a technique that was honed at gigs and in clubs as a sideman for the Isley Brothers, Jimi Hendrix broke through in London with his three-man supergroup, the Jimi Hendrix Experience. It is hard to imagine a greater, or more surreal, moment in guitar music than 9:00 a.m. on the Monday morning of 18 August 1969 in the Catskill Mountains, two hours northwest of New York City. Hendrix was scheduled to play the closing set of the Woodstock Music and Art Fair on Sunday night, but everything about the schedule was turned on its head by a combination of production incompetence on the part of the organizers and bad weather. Hendrix was unceremoniously bumped to close out the festival on Monday morning. Regardless, forty thousand people stayed to hear Hendrix play what was one of the most remarkable sets in the history of music. And thankfully every note of his incandescent playing was captured on film. Hendrix made his guitar not just the instrument of his music; he changed the way the guitar sounded. He changed the way the guitar was played. In a very real sense, Jimi Hendrix changed the world of rock music.

At the same moment, Jimmy Page had done something similar with Led Zeppelin but in a different way. Page was (and is) a virtuoso electric guitarist who had honed his skills in the recording studios of London as a guitarist for hire. Once in Led

Clarence Thomas, left, with his Martin D-28,
with the Byrds in 1971.

Johnny Ramone playing one of his Mosrite guitars in 1978.

Billie Eilish with FINNEAS playing his custom Fender Telecaster, 2021.

Zeppelin, with bandmates who perfectly echoed his theatrical instincts, Page's performative stage presence, combined with his virtuosity, created a new world of rock music art. In an unfortunate twist of popular culture, Page and Led Zeppelin also ushered in a world of hard guitar rock, which, in turn, gave the world the dubious delights of heavy metal, of macho, misogynistic bombast, of big hair and tight jeans, of Deep Purple and Black Sabbath. Of Ozzy Osbourne. Looked at from a contemporary perspective, heavy metal wilts under its own dead weight, and its often-great guitar playing with it. And the women of heavy metal the world over now ask themselves, "How did we put up with that?"

"Solos come and go. A great riff lasts forever." — Keith Richards

Although the guitar solo in "Stairway to Heaven" wasn't the first solo ever played, Page's playing seems to mark the beginning of the guitar solo as a musical phenomenon, a burst of guitar pyrotechnics in the middle of a rock song but having an existence separate from the song. There were great solos before "Stairway," of course, including virtually anything played by George Harrison, but it was the promotion of the solo from simply very good guitar playing to guitar heroics that both drove the phenomenon and became its weakest link. Rick Beato may be the most perceptive and musically sophisticated guitar commentator on the Internet. Beato's video "Top Twenty Rock Guitar Solos of All Time" is both instructive and entertaining, not least because Beato plays all the solos himself. His examples range from hair metal anthems by Eddie Van Halen to jazz-inflected lines from some of the best electric guitar players, including Steve Lukather and Larry Carlton. All of Beato's examples of great guitar solos span a relatively short time period, from 1965 and "Hey Joe" by Jimi Hendrix to 1982 and "Stone in Love" by Journey, which suggests that the "heroic" guitar solo played itself out, eventually becoming self-parody. However short-lived the phenomenon was, there is no denying the boomer romance attached to such solos as those in "Stairway to Heaven" and "Comfortably Numb," David Gilmour's anthem to muscle relaxants and Anglo-rock alienation.

While the grungy brilliance of Kurt Cobain eventually exposed the vapid buffonery of big-hair heavy metal, Jimi Hendrix's music did something utterly new. The gestural, performative quality of his Woodstock performance, and the recordings that he made when at his peak, opened the eyes and ears of a new generation of guitarists who were eager for any direction other than metal, on the one hand, or bubblegum pop, on the other. Punk flooded into this vacuum, ushered in by Hendrix and taken to new and greater heights by the Clash, the Ramones and, mercifully, by the brilliance of a young Dubliner whose guitar sound brought us, as if on a sonic dreamscape, to the end of the twentieth century. The band was U2, the guitarist was the Edge; the future looked brighter at last. With his slashing, echoing, repeating guitar figures, full of harmonic expression and spare chord voicings, the Edge—and contemporaries, including Johnny Marr of the Smiths—created not only a new sound for the guitar but a new role for the guitarist, one that is still being explored by the next generation of guitar heroes.

And so it has continued into the twenty-first century, the age of the Internet, of MIDI guitar sampling, of Pro Tools, and of MP3s and the Apple iPod, that brilliant invention of rock fan designer Jony Ive. It is a century that brought the end of the traditional record company and the beginning of streaming. Who and where are the contemporary guitar heroes?

It is a healthy landscape, to be sure. On the one hand we have FINNEAS, either on his own or with his sister Billie Eilish, herself an excellent guitar and ukulele player. Mitch Rowland,

creating superb sounds for Harry Styles, is another kind of guitar hero, one who doesn't feel the need to shred. For her part, Taylor Swift's rhythmic acoustic guitar playing demands comparison to Joni Mitchell and, it is not fanciful to suggest, to the syncopated rhythms of Keith Richards. These guitarists are keeping their virtuosity quiet, allowing the melodies to shine.

At the other edges of new, digital rock guitar music are unquestionably great players such as Tosin Abasi and Misha Mansoor, whose polyphonic hyperdexterity seems to bring OG metal and progressive rock bands such as Yes back to life. Is there an absence of lyrical line, of space, in this playing? Without a doubt. Only time will tell if it can mature into something great.

Popular Culture

Consider the opening chord of the Beatles' 1964 song "A Hard Day's Night." Although the song was released almost six decades ago, music fans still obsess about the chord. Musicologists lecture about it, online fans use computer programs to simulate the wave form of each note, and guitarists play it. Competing theories abound: what chord is it, exactly, and who played it? For the record, it's an old-fashioned Fadd9, played by George Harrison, John Lennon, Paul McCartney (striking one D note on his bass), and George Martin (playing the chord on a Steinway grand piano). Ringo adds a single drum beat for good measure. That there is so much chatter about just one single chord that is almost sixty years old is a sign of just how pervasive the guitar is in the popular imagination, not to mention how relevant the Beatles continue to be, not only as a band but as guitar innovators.

The guitar strides through pop culture like no other musical instrument, as it has done, it seems, since the time of Antonio Stradivari. The great Dutch master Johannes Vermeer was a contemporary of Stradivari, although the two men lived worlds apart—one in Delft, in the Netherlands, the other in the Italian city of Cremona, in what was then Lombardy. But there, in one of Vermeer's most celebrated paintings, is a young lady strumming a guitar that, if not a Stradivari masterpiece, looks to be a short-scale, five-course guitar of great quality and beauty. The young lady is a

wealthy young Dutch woman, very much of her time, and she is playing the guitar rather than the ancient lute, which Vermeer had also painted. This was a strong signal that the very modern guitar had found a secure place in the popular imagination—a cool and hip instrument for an elegant young lady-about-town to own and play.

The late Baroque period was a time of increasing personal freedom; a time of ideas, of science, and of increasing technology; a time when the secular was finding a place alongside the sacred in the popular imagination. Painting, sculpture, and music were the pop cultures of the Baroque and Renaissance. Although the piano was born in the Baroque era, the guitar was portable and easier to play, and it quickly found its place in the fancier parlors of Europe. Judging by the high quality of the guitars of the time, it was clearly an instrument for the well-to-do. Jan Molenaar, who is believed to have been a student of Frans Hals, featured a guitar, a fancy lute, and a cello in his most famous painting of a handsome and wealthy Dutch family playing music. Once again, the instruments are at the fore, signifiers, as if they were needed, given the quality of the fashions being worn, of the general wealth of the family.

As art turned toward portraiture in the late eighteenth and early nineteenth centuries, painters increasingly used the guitar as an easily identifiable signifier in their work. The greatest of the English society painters, Joshua Reynolds, frequently used the guitar, usually played by a noblewoman, in his portraits. The guitar was a seductive object even then. It connoted passion and a private, perhaps elite, skill. This private side of guitar is at one with its small size and low volume. This was an instrument for private pleasure. That the guitars were often expensively designed and built made them attractive to a certain type of wealthy enthusiast.

Niccolò Paganini was not only the greatest violinist of his era; he also played and taught the guitar. And just as the ladies of high society commissioned portraits with their guitars, high-society ladies engaged the best, most famous teachers. Paganini's star pupil was the grand duchess of Tuscany, Elisa Bonaparte Baciocchi, Napoleon Bonaparte's sister. Elisa was not only Paganini's student; she was also apparently his lover. In Elisa's hands, her guitar was not just an instrument of private pleasure; it was an illicit pleasure, too.

The Pre-Raphaelite painters hated Joshua Reynolds, whom they called Sir Sloschua, believing him to have betrayed the great rigor of the early Renaissance masters, Raphael and Michelangelo. Their approach to painting was rigorous and expressive, and intensely, excessively romantic. The heroes were manly, the heroines comely, and the latter often played guitars. Pre-Raphaelite painting, like much nineteenth-century art, was saccharine sweet and impossibly rooted in anything but the real world. Just as the bubblegum pop and glam rock of the 1970s was inevitably replaced by punk, nineteenth-century art was bound to implode. And it did, thankfully, with the arrival of the twentieth century and modernism.

In the early twentieth century, Pablo Picasso and Georges Braque traded pictures back and forth in Paris as their experiments in Cubism developed

The Guitar Player, Johannes Vermeer, 1672.

Family Making Music, Jan Molenaar, c.1636.

Sorrow and Song, Edmund Blair Leighton, 1893.

Woman with Guitar, Pablo Picasso, 1924.

The Beatles' rooftop concert in London, 30 January 1969. Paul McCartney plays his Hofner 500/1 Bass, John Lennon his favorite Epiphone Casino, and George Harrison a new custom Fender Rosewood Telecaster.

into a full-fledged competition. Each of these great artists loved to feature the guitar, and it is easy to see how seductive the guitar was for an artist. The very shape of the guitar is a metaphor, with its feminine waist and long neck. As challenging as the guitar is to represent in perspective, with its curves and intersecting lines, it can also be broken up and remain recognizable. Picasso and Braque proved that point over and over again.

The guitar was a totem, a representation of an attitude. It was modern, popular, and, since the earliest times, a little subversive. It was perfect for the new, modernist world of the early 1900s, a world soon to be connected by the latest technology of radio. Radio itself was, and continues to be a century later, a perfect medium for popular music. The blues, and its sophisticated sister, jazz, grew alongside the growth of radio, music recording, and movies. Jazz was all about cool and entertainment. Big bands were the medium; the guitar was a little buried.

The 1930s were the height of the jazz age, an age of what has come to be known as the Great American Songbook. The guitar was, along with the piano, often playing the song, but it was finding it hard to be heard, and in popular culture, the guitar missed out on the jazz age. Instead, it became a highly visible cowboy instrument, an accessory to a legion of cowboy movie stars who rode the plains and sang the high, lonesome songs of the not-yet-there country music. Roy Rogers, Gene Autry, Tex Ritter, and Bob Steele all starred in corny, B-grade cactus 'n' cattle cowboy genre movies, always with guitars, always singing.

Known as the Country Gentleman, Chet Atkins was an up-and-coming guitar player, and Gretsch wanted him to endorse a guitar. Their first efforts tapped into just this cowboy corniness, and Chet was having none of it. In the end Atkins allowed a cowboy-style cattle brand in the shape of his initials, C. A., to adorn the lower body of the guitar, but it was short-lived and disappeared completely within a year.

As the twentieth century matured, so did the guitar, and it developed into one of the key graphic images of pop culture. This was helped by it becoming the great solo instrument of pop; loud and sexy, it entrenched itself firmly in the graphics, the literature, and the music of the time.

Elvis Presley took the singing cowboy idea and turned it on its head. The great musicals of the earlier part of the twentieth century had largely ignored the guitar, but no one could ignore Elvis, or the movies he made in the 1950s and 1960s. Elvis was a huge, worldwide phenomenon, a great singer, and a very good guitar player who only looked average because he played alongside Scotty Moore, one of the true greats of postwar American rock guitarists. Elvis had a way of posing, with or without his guitar, that made his image a curious contradiction of both sexual danger and apple-pie sweetness. Elvis was everything the viewer wanted him to be—cute, sexy, bad in the best way—and he was everywhere.

Love Me Tender, in 1956, was Elvis's first movie, and he was a star from the start. On every movie poster everywhere in the world, Elvis had a guitar slung around his shoulders. And in virtually every movie he was in, he had songs to sing. Some of the movies were great, such as *Jailhouse Rock*, which was, and remains, a movie classic. Others were clunkers. But Elvis's performance, as both an actor and a singer, was never less than interesting and was often very, very good. Elvis somehow defined the 1950s and a postwar liberation that presaged the actual social, sexual, and musical liberations of the 1960s. Although Elvis's addictions ushered a long and slow decline, his impact on popular culture, with his guitar ever present and inextricably bound to his image, cannot be understated. Elvis was the first snake-hipped popular guitar hero.

The Beatles were the first true guitar band, and their look dominated the imagery of the 1960s. Four men—three with guitars and a drummer—all with long hair and sharp suits. The Beatles were cool because they were young, famous, and exquisitely talented. Above all, the Beatles redefined cool, shifting the world's gaze away from the American version—the Elvis version—and redirecting it toward Carnaby Street and London. The Brit explosion had begun.

The 1967 album cover for *Sgt. Pepper's Lonely Hearts Club Band* took pop imagery to a new level, embracing mainstream art in a design by contemporary English pop artist Peter Blake. Young music fans carried these albums from one friend's house to another, poring over the imagery, smelling the ink, breathing in the liner notes. The sound of the Beatles' guitar-driven music was in the air, floating from windows, from storefronts, from factories and offices.

The 1969 *Abbey Road* album became one of the most powerful images of the 1960s. John Lennon dressed in a perfect, tailor-made white suit. Paul went barefoot, in his own perfectly tailored suit. George wore denim bell-bottoms. The image went around the world and affected not just the way people looked; it changed everything from music to cars to food to attitudes.

Two guitar players took the industry of graphic design surrounding rock music and came to redefine the guitar in pop culture. Eric Clapton joined with Ginger Baker on drums and Jack Bruce on bass to form Cream in 1966. They chose the name Cream because they considered themselves to be the "cream" of British blues musicians at the time. Eric Clapton created guitar lines that felt as if they could be played by anyone, and everyone tried. As Clapton's solos became famous, other guitarists locked onto the idea of a bravura showcase in the middle of a song. Peter Green, Fleetwood Mac's guitar virtuoso

Arnold Skolnick's poster for Woodstock, August 1969.

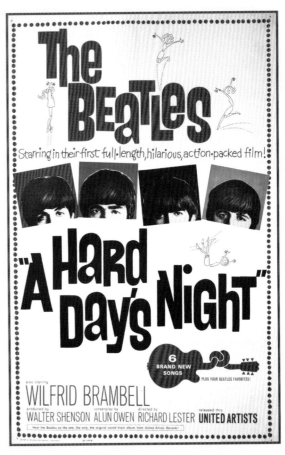

Clockwise from top left: poster for Elvis Presley's 1956 acting debut in *Love Me Tender*; poster for *A Hard Day's Night*, the Beatles movie that changed the sound of rock music; program cover design for the American Live Aid concert, 13 July 1985.

Its double neck held vertically, Jimmy Page plays his Gibson EDS-1275. This was how Page played the twelve-string part of "Stairway to Heaven" in concert.

who left the band in 1970, created quiet solo lines of aching beauty. Jeff Beck, brilliant and irascible—so much so that the Yardbirds threw him out of their band—couldn't quite decide what kind of guitar hero he wanted to be.

And then there was Jimmy Page. Page was a session musician in London (he handed out business cards advertising the fact) before he joined Led Zeppelin and became the other most famous guitarist in the world. Page was Clapton's equal as a guitar virtuoso, and he had something else. He had poise, and he could pose. He played his guitar with the neck vertical, his knee high, and his boyishly beautiful face perfectly calm. The whole image became indelibly linked to the idea of a guitar hero playing solo: phallic, macho, undeniably sexy. Add drugs to the mix, and the psychedelic, guitar-led pop graphics of the 1970s came to define the imagery for two decades.

This frantic rock energy was exploding from London and changing everything from Pop art to advertising and graphic design; however, on the other side of the Atlantic, folk music was bursting out of the coffee shops of Greenwich Village in New York City and into mainstream popular consciousness. Bob Dylan and Joan Baez were competitors and opposites—and for a time, even lovers. Dylan's louche personal style emerged, more or less completely formed, from the pages of a Jack Kerouac novel or an Allen Ginsberg poem, read in protest on the steps of some college. The guitar was ever present. Joan Baez's sweet soprano voice could have come straight from a convent, but it was built on a moral framework of stainless steel, and her message was powerful. Again, the guitar was ever present in Baez's case, spawning a special series of New York Martin guitars, small and easy to play but with steel strings so they could be heard above the clink of glasses.

Two of the greatest guitar heroes of this era, Jimi Hendrix and Pete Townshend, in their performative playing, destroyed the very guitars they played. Hendrix famously poured lighter fuel on his Stratocaster and set it alight. Townshend preferred to smash his guitar on the stage. Both images fueled the antiestablishment aura around the guitar and became indelible totems for a generation fed up with what had gone before. These attitudes fueled, in turn, a new wave of music, first in New York and then in London. Raucous, loud, with guitars often out of tune, punk's attitudes and sounds reverberate still. The Clash and the Sex Pistols were everything and everywhere, the most urgent of bands, screaming their musical presence and relishing their infamy with frantic energy. In New York, the Ramones, taking their names from Paul McCartney's hotel pseudonym, Paul Ramon, blew through acceptable, middle-of-the-road radio music with a force unheard before. The Ramones played and toured and toured and played, relentlessly and brilliantly, and took a generation on the road with them.

Although punk music was not about the guitar, it could not have existed without the guitar, and the pervading image is of a low-slung ax, hammered at the knees to within an inch of its life. Punk entrepreneur Malcolm McLaren was the Svengali to the Sex Pistols, forming them, shaping their look and their sound. McLaren, with Vivienne Westwood as his fashion designer alter ego, also shaped the imagery of London punk. With their protégés changing the sound of music, McLaren and Westwood hovered high above the world of punk, creating and refining pop culture. The images and album covers of the time remain fresh and endlessly relevant, such as the Clash's *London Calling* and the Sex Pistols' *Never Mind the Bollocks, Here's the Sex Pistols* and their "God Save the Queen" single.

Two different movements of guitar music—one a direct response to the other—saw out the twentieth century while also defining the popular culture of their time. Less influential was heavy

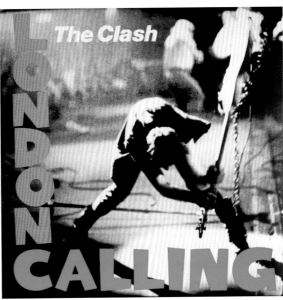

Bob Dylan and Joan Baez singing a duet, one of many they would perform between 1961 and 1965.

Pennie Smith's photograph from The Clash's 1979 concert in New York became one of the defining images of punk rock.

metal, also known simply as metal, which grew directly out of the big-hair imagery of Robert Plant and Jimmy Page, both of Led Zeppelin. Metal bands drilled down on the cliché of sex, drugs, and rock 'n' roll to the point of living, and dying, by their musical lifestyles. The imagery was overt: sexist and supremacist, with naked ladies, skulls, crossbones, Teutonic crosses, and iron crosses everywhere. With increasing silliness and crudity, from the music to the iconography, metal couldn't last. As if ushered by the gods, Seattle's grunge pretty much killed it, without quite driving a stake through its heart. Presiding grunge philosopher Kurt Cobain—and his guitar-led band, Nirvana—remained at the center of the music. The grunge movement, founded in the coffee shops of Seattle, came to dominate fashion, art, graphics, and, yes, even body art—tattoos—well into the twenty-first century. If it appropriated shamelessly from punk, it didn't care. Grunge had the same attitudes, similar heroes and heroines, and was, and remains, beyond cool.

That the guitar and guitarist are truly the drivers of twentieth-century pop culture can be found in the lists of *Rolling Stone* magazine. Among their most popular lists is "100 Greatest Guitarists." Every single guitarist is from a twentieth-century band, as if the boomer definition of a rock star is somehow frozen, along with the music, firmly in the last century. Only half of the top ten guitarists in the *Rolling Stone's* list are still playing, while the number one player, Jimi Hendrix, died more than half a century ago, in 1970.

The guitar as a pop-culture phenomenon suffered in the early years of the twenty-first century as popular music, driven by rap and hip-hop, became a product of computers, MIDI sampling, Pro Tools production methods, and keyboards. But the guitar, even if it was a little down, is emphatically not out. Contemporary guitarists/

Kurt Cobain, pictured in 1991, helped rescue American rock music from the ravages of big-hair heavy metal.

Taylor Swift is seen here playing her custom Gibson Les Paul on the Red tour in 2013.

songwriters Taylor Swift, Jack Antonoff of the Bleachers, and Aaron Dessner of the National are some of the best musicians of any era, and they could hardly be more famous, even if they play in a completely different style than the big-hair heroes of yesteryear. The new guitar heroes are more cerebral, less wildly rebellious, and conscious of their widely differing visual styles. Guitar heroism has now become as much a product of social media and Internet memes as of the grungy basement clubs of the past. Bright and wide-eyed, contemporary guitarists have tattoos designed by well-known artists, the ink indelibly part of the image. It is such a far cry from the twentieth century and the quaint imagery of boomer rock. The late, and greatly lamented, Stephen Fitzpatrick of the duo Her's was pushing his music, and his contextual style of electric guitar playing, in hitherto unheard-of directions. We will never know exactly how great Fitzpatrick really was. Canadian indie guitarists Neil Smith and Christopher Vanderkooy, of the band Peach Pit, have channeled the jangly guitar sounds of the Byrds for the twenty-first century, and with them the carefully styled imagery of post-grunge. And the Californian guitarist Steve Lacy describes his music in visual terms, as "tartan plaid."

Three guitarists have emerged as popular Internet commentators, each propelling the guitar to the center of virtual experience. Rick Beato's YouTube channel, in which he dives deep into the musical theory of guitar playing, has millions of viewers. Beato brings the greatest contemporary players as his guests, running the gamut from Joni Mitchell, who is at last being celebrated for her guitar brilliance, to contemporary guitar shredders Tosin Abasi and Tim Henson. Henson, from the band Polyphia, has coined the phrase "boomer bends" to describe Eric Clapton's style of playing, with its singing, wide vibrato. That style is now faintly ridiculed by these new young shredders. Mary Spender is a classically trained guitarist and singer/

songwriter, whose YouTube explorations on pop music and technology have become required viewing. Meanwhile, Chris Buck's YouTube show, Friday Fretworks, not only shows off his virtuoso playing, he enlightens his audience with perceptive insights into guitar playing and guitars from all eras of guitar rock music.

The guitar in pop culture now sits firmly on the Internet, whether played on streaming and playlist sites or celebrated by guitarist commentators. For these, led by Beato, and including English guitarists Buck and Spender, the guitar is still a vibrant instrument of not only popular music but of contemporary popular culture. Guitar fans in every corner of our Internet world wholeheartedly agree.

Guitars

Antonio Stradivari
The Hill
1688

Type and body: Baroque guitar with five string courses. Spruce top with maple back and sides.
Neck and Fingerboard: Walnut neck. Oak fingerboard.

Born in Cremona, Italy, into a family of master instrument makers, in about 1644, Antonio Stradivari was the most celebrated luthier of his day. Stradivari signed his instruments in a Latin style, Antonius Stradivarius, and it is by this name that both he and especially his violins are still sometimes known today.

Stradivari lived a long and productive life, producing thousands of instruments of which a great many survive and are played. His violins are best known, played by the greatest players and attracting large sums at auction. Less well-known are his guitars, of which only a handful survive.

Only two Stradivari guitars are thought to be completely original: the Hill and the Rawlins. The Hill, at the Ashmolean Museum in Oxford, England, was named after the Hill company of luthiers in London, which was for generations the most important authority on Stradivari violins in the world. The Rawlins is part of the extraordinary collection of the National Music Museum in Vermillion, South Dakota.

The Hill guitar has some features unusual for an Italian guitar, whose styles were greatly influenced by the Venetian tradition of highly ornate instruments. Almost austere in appearance, this Stradivari is in the Spanish tradition, as if Stradivari was trying to identify with his more serious Spanish counterparts rather than the florid Venetian stylists some 155 miles (250 km) to the east. With a two-piece spruce top and abundant use of maple, the guitar looks almost modern in appearance, except perhaps for its large head, which accommodates five courses of strings.

Only one of Stradivari's guitars, the so-called Sabionari from 1697, is still played. While purists wince at the thought of an ultra-rare Stradivari guitar being restored to playable condition, it is a spine-tingling feeling to hear how a Stradivari guitar actually sounds.

It is fun to imagine the kind of music that might have been played on the Hill guitar. Madrigals, simple folk tunes, perhaps, or something altogether more serious. Santiago de Murcia was a Spanish composer and a contemporary of Stradivari. Murcia's "Tarantella" is now part of the canon of classical guitar songs. Norwegian Rolf Lislevand, who specializes in early music, has played the Sabionari Strad, and his exuberant playing of the famous "Tarantella" can be seen and heard at various streaming sites online.

John Preston Guitar 1770

Type and body: Six-course, steel-string acoustic
English guitar. Spruce top. Maple body.
Body: Rosewood body with spruce top
Neck and Fingerboard: Maple neck. "Ebonized"
maple fingerboard.

The basic shape of the guitar had been settled for centuries, but that didn't stop English luthiers from going their own way. The English guitar, or cittern, has the pear shape of a lute but is a much simpler instrument with a flat top and back instead of the intricately made backs of the lute or the mandolin, which were made by gluing together curved ribs or staves.

The English guitar was extremely popular and was as likely to be seen and heard played by titled ladies in genteel parlors as by rowdy minstrels in boisterous taverns. It was simply made, robust, and portable, and the sound from its steel strings could cut through a murmuring crowd. It had the kind of popularity that acoustic and Spanish guitars have today, leaning against teenage beds and on drawing room couches. It was clearly a treasured a possession, judging by the number of times it appears in society portraits of the seventeenth and eighteenth centuries.

This late-eighteenth-century guitar was made by John Preston at his workshop in Long Acre in London. Preston was the leading luthier in England during this period of the English guitar's popularity, and his instruments were intricate and beautifully made. This guitar has a spruce top with maple back and neck and an interesting built-in capo made of ebony and brass. It also features Preston's unique "watchkey" tuners, also made of brass, which are still used on the Portuguese guitar, the modern descendent of the English guitar. Preston's major rival in London was the German luthier John Frederick Hintz, who also claimed to be the inventor of this type of tuning device.

To understand the kind of music that might have been played on an English guitar, it is worth listening to folk singer Andy Irvine. Irvine's playing of harmonic continuo lines underneath a folk song's melody was a feature of early folk bands such as Sweeney's Men and later Planxty. Although Irvine played a bouzouki, his beautiful playing on the folk tune "Willie O' Winsbury" is evocative of the music that would have been heard played on the English guitar.

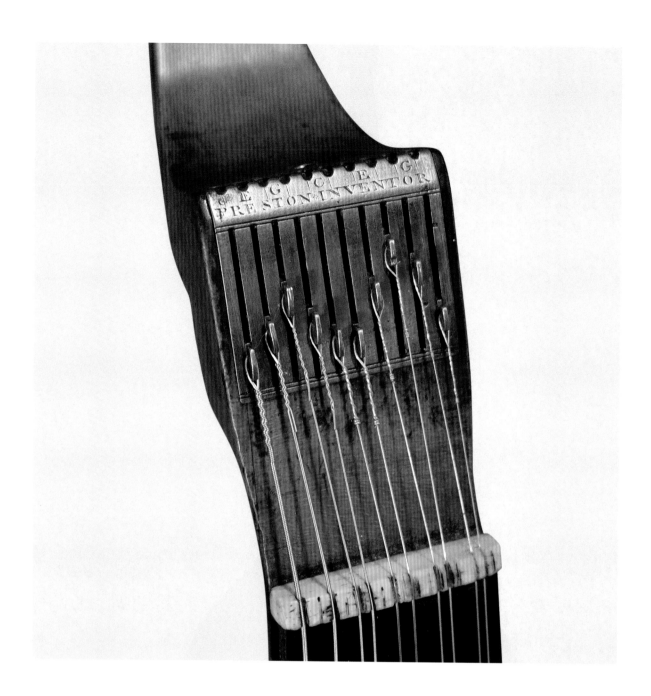

Guitars

Louis Panormo Guitar 1823

Type and body: Spanish classical acoustic guitar.
Spruce top. Maple body.
Neck and Fingerboard: Maple headstock.
Mahogany neck. Brazilian rosewood fingerboard.

The great Catalan virtuoso Fernando Sor moved to London in 1815, where, over the course of eight years, he built a famous career as a recitalist, teacher, and composer. Sor brought with him the Spanish guitar, which supplanted the English guitar in popularity, especially among the hipper, wealthier Londoner concertgoers and guitar fans.

The son of a well-known Italian luthier, Louis Panormo did very well making high-quality stringed instruments from his studio in Blooms-bury, in central London. Indeed, Panormo claimed on his labels to be "the only maker of guitars in the Spanish style" working in England. That Spanish style may have come from Fernando Sor, who introduced Panormo to the work of the Pagés brothers from Cadiz, Spain. Panormo's designs are close to those of the Pagés brothers, especially in the body, with a shape and size that are virtually identical to those of the brothers.

The neck and head, however, are the truest marks of Panormo's design brilliance. Panormo used brass machine tuners on his heads, and perhaps worried that, with the extra weight, these would overbalance the guitar, he sought to lighten the head by carving an open, airy design. Without precedent in any Spanish guitar up to that point, Panormo carved his head from a piece of maple that was joined to a mahogany neck, knowing that the maple would be at once both strong and light enough to accommodate the brass tuners. Panormo's guitar business boomed, partly due to the quality of his guitars and partly, perhaps, in response to the demand brought on by Fernando Sor's fame. Sor himself preferred to play guitars by other makers, including his eventual favorite, the great French luthier René Lacôte in Paris.

Modern English luthier Gary Southwell believes Panormo to have been the greatest nineteenth-century guitar maker of all, and he has re-created one of Panormo's designs as part of his own range of classical guitars.

Johann Stauffer Romantic Guitar c.1840

Type and body: Hollow-body acoustic guitar.
Spruce top. Maple back and sides.
Neck and Fingerboard: Laminated neck.
Rosewood fingerboard.

Just as London-based Louis Panormo was greatly influenced by Fernando Sor, Viennese luthier Johann Georg Stauffer was influenced by the great Italian guitarist and composer Luigi Rinaldo Legnani. It was more than an influence, however, because Legnani essentially showed Stauffer what he wanted. This was completely acknowledged by Stauffer, whose labels bore the legend "Nach dem Modell des Luigi Legnani" ("Based on the model of Luigi Legnani").

Stauffer's guitar is a striking design and establishes the six-string arrangement that we see to this day. Whereas Panormo was using a modern fan-bracing technique to support the soundboard, or top, of the guitar, Stauffer's innovations lay elsewhere. He was the first to have the extended fingerboard elevated over the body of the guitar; he arranged the six single strings to run in parallel lines straight to the tuners; the tuners themselves were mounted on an ornately carved headstock; and the shafts and gears of the tuners were kept in place by a brass plate attached to the rear of the headstock. All of these innovations would have a

great bearing on subsequent acoustic guitar design, both in Europe and the United States.

The body of the guitar is elegantly symmetric, with a large sound hole and a signature mustache bridge. The top is made of spruce, while maple is used for the sides and the back. And whereas Panormo used expensive ebony and rosewood for his fingerboards, Stauffer used a less expensive laminate.

Perhaps Stauffer's greatest design move was to hire the young German Christian Frederick Martin to be his apprentice. Martin would eventually become Stauffer's workshop foreman before emigrating to the United States, where he founded C. F. Martin & Co., now the world's oldest guitar company. During their time working together in Vienna, Stauffer and Martin were laying the design foundations of what would become the ubiquitous modern acoustic guitar. Yet, while Martin went on to thrive in the New World, Stauffer, along with his business, and for all his importance in the history of guitar design, fell into a slow, sad decline.

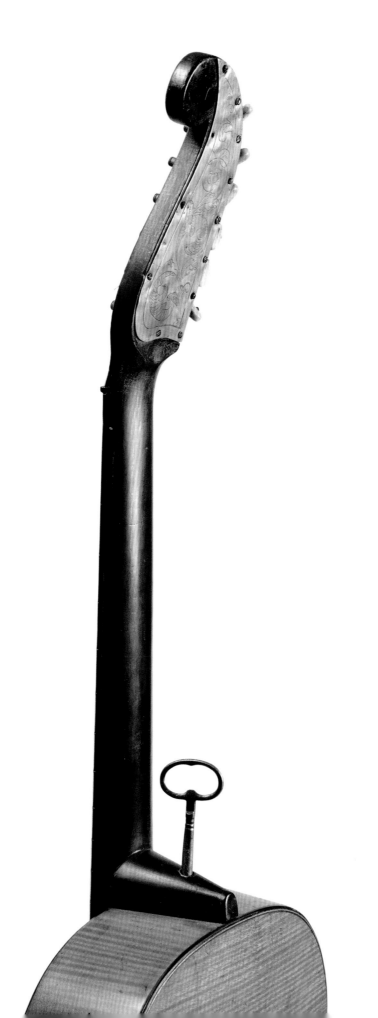

Antonio de Torres Jurado Parlor Guitar 1883

Type and body: Classical acoustic guitar.
Spruce top. Brazilian rosewood back and sides.
Neck and Fingerboard: Cedar neck. Ebony
fingerboard.

Thanks to Fernando Sor's fame, both as a player and as a composer, the Spanish guitar was, by the middle of the nineteenth century, completely established as a concert instrument and played by celebrity guitarists. The demand for top-class instruments was strong. The greatest luthier of this period, and the maker who more than any other established the style of the modern classical Spanish guitar, was the Seville maker Antonio de Torres Jurado.

Torres was such a great guitar maker that his oeuvre is generally divided into two eras, or "epochs." His first great flourish was from his workshop in Seville, where he produced guitars that were, by any standard, nearly perfect. One of the first and most important moves that Torres made was to increase the size of the body. Up to this point, guitars had slender, symmetrical bodies, with the upper and lower sections, called bouts, more or less the same size. Torres enlarged the body, giving more depth to the lower bout. This changed the sound beyond anything that had been heard previously, giving a sonorous depth to the

bass notes without losing any clarity in the upper register of the guitar.

Torres eschewed ornamentation for its own sake. This was the middle of the nineteenth century, and, by our standards, the guitars seem minimalist, modernist, plain; they look as if they might have been made a century later.

Francisco Tárrega was the greatest guitar virtuoso of his time, and he played a Torres guitar. Tárrega's patronage of Torres was of great mutual benefit. Tárrega's audiences surely knew that they were listening to the best guitarist in the world, playing the best guitar.

Washburn
Style 205 Parlor Guitar
c.1895

Type and body: Acoustic guitar. Spruce top.
Rosewood back and sides.
Neck and Fingerboard: Presumed mahogany
neck. Ebony fingerboard.

With the obvious exception of the electric guitar, it could be said that all guitars are parlor guitars, because they are designed to be played in domestic or private rooms. Parlor guitars are small instruments, and since they are plucked or strummed rather than bowed, their ability to project volume is limited. Nevertheless, while acoustic guitars have continued to grow in size and in volume since the end of the nineteenth century, the smaller so-called parlor guitars have held their own.

Based in Chicago, Washburn was among the first of the successful American guitar makers. It was a big manufacturer of musical instruments, and guitars made up just one line in its catalog. This guitar, the 205, taken from a line of guitars with varying degrees of size and price, was designed to be marketed to women players and was described as a parlor guitar. It is a finely made, small-bodied, short-scale guitar, with mother-of-pearl adornments that are both eye-catching and expensive to produce. The overall design sought to appeal to well-to-do guitar players, which presumably, in this case, would be women.

The shape of this guitar is slimmer and more symmetrical than the predominant shapes of either the classical Spanish guitar or the emerging American acoustic guitars of Martin and Gibson. Indeed, Washburn guitars sounded great, and they were the main rival to Martin at the end of the nineteenth century and into the twentieth.

The Washburn company faded away as the jazz age brought larger, louder guitars, which came to define the style of the American guitar in the first half of the twentieth century, even if the surviving guitars are highly collectible today.

José Ramírez Classical Guitar 1897

Type and body: Flamenco acoustic guitar. Spruce top. Cypress back and sides.
Neck and Fingerboard: Cedar neck. Brazilian rosewood fingerboard.

The name Ramírez has a revered place in the history of guitar making. Founded in Madrid in 1882 by José Ramírez and his younger brother, Manuel, the Ramírez business has been built around beautiful guitars for classical and flamenco players.

The Ramírez name is also renowned for a feud between the two brothers that almost overshadows their many triumphs. Early in their partnership, Manuel planned to set up a shop in Paris, with José's apparent support. Instead, Manuel set up a shop in Madrid that was in direct competition with José. After the split, each of the brothers made a significant impact on the design of the traditional, Torres-style Spanish guitar.

For José, the Tablao, first made in 1913, was a masterpiece—a larger, brighter, louder guitar, ideal for flamenco players, who were, above all, bravura accompanists of flamenco singers and dancers.

Manuel's designs had a lightness, too, with a bright tone and a sustain that was perfect for classical players. One such player was a young Andrés Segovia. When Manuel first heard Segovia play, he pulled a used guitar from his stock and gave it to the young virtuoso. Segovia played that guitar for the next twenty-five years. It is now in the collection of the Metropolitan Museum of Art in New York.

This guitar was made by José early in his career and is a perfect example of the Ramírez style, with spruce top, cypress back and sides, a Brazilian rosewood fingerboard, and a mother-of-pearl rosette bordering the large sound hole.

Enrique Garcia
Guitar
1912

Type and body: Classical acoustic guitar.
Spruce top. Brazilian rosewood back and sides.
Neck and Fingerboard: Mahogany neck.
Ebony fingerboard.

A direct line runs from the great nineteenth-century maker Antonio de Torres Jurado to the Ramírez brothers, José and Manuel, to Enrique Garcia, who, while working for José Ramírez, became famous for the quality of his designs. Working under Ramírez, it was Garcia's guitar that won a gold medal at the World's Columbian Exposition of 1893 in Chicago, which attracted huge attention both in Spain and internationally. José Ramírez made full use of Garcia's victory in his marketing.

With this success, it was inevitable that Garcia would set up his own shop. He did so in 1895 by moving to Barcelona, where he became known as the originator of the Catalan school of guitar making. By the turn of the twentieth century, he was one of the leading guitar makers in the world. Garcia traded on his renown, especially in South America and, in particular, in Buenos Aires.

His influence on Catalan guitar making was profound. Garcia taught two great luthiers, Francisco Simplicio and Ignacio Fleta. Together, they made an enormous impact on guitar making in the twentieth century, and their influence is still felt in classical guitar and in flamenco.

This guitar is thought to be from Garcia's late work. The elongated sound hole is a brilliant stroke, but there is some doubt if it was made by Garcia himself or by a later hand, possibly after a repair at the Buenos Aires shop of Antigua Casa Nuñez. Either way, it is a beautiful guitar from a master.

Gibson Style O 1918

Type and body: Archtop acoustic guitar.
Spruce top. Birch back and sides.
Neck and Fingerboard: Mahogany neck.
Ebony fingerboard.

The word *genius* has lost so much of its meaning in these postmodern days that it is not sufficient to describe Orville Gibson, the founder of Gibson guitars and the designer/builder of this guitar, the Gibson Model O (for the oval sound hole).

The original guitar had a simple, handwritten label:

"The Gibson
Mandolins & Guitars
Patented Feb 1st, 1898
Made by OH Gibson
Kalamazoo"

So much is embedded in those words: let's start with mandolins and guitars. Up to this point, mandolins had been made, like lutes, with strips of wood called staves, glued together to form a curved back. Instead, Gibson carved the top and back of his mandolins from two single pieces of wood, and the success of this technique, combined with the overall quality of his instruments, as good as killed the manufacture of traditional mandolins in the United States.

Applying the same carving technique to guitars, Gibson effectively created the archtop guitar, a form that came to be the standard, especially for jazz and big band players, for the next fifty years. The beauty of a carved top is that it obviates the need to use complicated bracing to stiffen the top against the strain of the strings under tension. And the extra volume created by the carved top gives a nice boost to volume without losing tone.

Gibson's genius came at an apparent cost to his mental health. He worked at arm's length from the Gibson company for a number of years and was hospitalized several times until his eventual death in 1918 at the age of sixty-two.

The guitar in this picture is the slightly later Style O with the mandolin curl on the shoulder, which creates an effective double cutaway, the first time a cutaway of any kind was featured on an acoustic guitar.

Weissenborn
Style 4
1920s

Type and body: Hawaiian lap steel guitar.
Koa top, back, and sides.
Neck and Fingerboard: One-piece koa hollow
neck and fingerboard.

The American obsession with Hawaiian music can be dated to one event: the 1915 Panama-Pacific International Exposition in San Francisco. It was there that performances by Hawaiian musicians sparked a huge surge in interest in all things Pacific, especially Hawaiian. With the portamento swoops of its slide guitars, typically played on steel-string acoustic guitars with the strings raised off the fingerboard, the music felt romantic and exotic, redolent of palm trees and ocean breezes. By sliding a steel bar over the steel strings, musicians were able to create the swooping figures that captured that Hawaiian sound.

Into this arena came two luthiers in Los Angeles. The first, Norwegian Chris Knutsen, was best known for harp guitars, but he responded to the demand for Hawaiian guitars by creating sometimes crude, lap steel guitars made of koa wood and spruce. The second luthier was Hermann Weissenborn, who was born in Germany but emigrated first to New York when he was in his mid-thirties and then to Los Angeles in his early forties. Weissenborn trained as a luthier in

Germany, and although he certainly knew Knutsen and was aware of—and in some ways inspired by—Knutsen's work, Weissenborn's own guitars were greatly superior in every way.

Made entirely of koa, and featuring a neck that is completely hollow, a Knutsen innovation, the Weissenborn is a guitar that can be played only on the lap. In one way this is unfortunate, because the great beauty of the guitar is hidden from the listener.

The rich, sweet sound of the Weissenborn is partly due to the hollow neck, which extends the body of the guitar all the way to the headstock. The Weissenborn was very successful, with guitars sold in large numbers all over the country. However, the death knell for the all-koa guitar came from National's metal resonator guitars, invented in Los Angeles by Hawaiian guitar player and showman George Beauchamp, along with entrepreneur and inventor John Dopyera. The National single-cone and tricone resophonic guitars were much louder than the Weissenborn and could be heard over other instruments, a distinct advantage over the all-wood acoustic Weissenborn.

The Folk Music Center in Claremont, California, is a music store and museum that has been at the heart of folk music and guitar playing in this part of Southern California since 1958. One frequent visitor to the store was guitarist David Lindley. Lindley has been a champion of the Weissenborn guitar for many years, with one of the largest collections of Weissenborns in the world. Lindley's frequent collaborations with his friend Ry Cooder have produced some of the best slide guitar music ever recorded, including "Mercury Blues," with Cooder playing a Stratocaster and Lindley a 1920s Weissenborn.

Stromberg-Voisinet Hawaiian Guitar 1920s

Type and body: Hawaiian-style slide guitar. Mahogany top, back, and sides.
Neck and Fingerboard: Plastic pearloid fingerboard.

Before it came to be known as the Kay Musical Instrument Company in 1931, Stromberg-Voisinet was one of the leading guitar and mandolin makers of the 1920s, the so-called roaring twenties. Making a range of mandolins, tenor guitars (four-string guitars), and beautifully shaped Venetian acoustic guitars, Stromberg-Voisinet was a maker of inexpensive, mass-market instruments.

In developing a guitar for the huge interest in Hawaiian music, Stromberg-Voisinet created a stunning example that leaned heavily on perceived images and ideas of the Pacific Islands, especially the swaying palm trees. Musically, there are two types of Hawaiian guitars. The first is the slide guitar, which is placed on the lap and played with a steel bar or tube that can create the portamento slides of notes and chords familiar to listeners as Hawaiian music. The opening swoop of the *Merrie Melodies* cartoon series was recorded in 1931 on a Hawaiian slide guitar by Los Angeles guitarist Freddie Tavares, who later joined Leo Fender and is generally credited as the design talent behind the Stratocaster.

The other style of Hawaiian guitar was designed to be played in a slack-key and open tuning, with two or three of the lower strings tuned down to create an open chord, often G major. The player then played Hawaiian songs in a loose fingerstyle that was hugely popular in the United States.

The Stromberg-Voisinet was a small parlor guitar that was very successful for this market. It came with an extravagantly imagined scene of palm trees on the body of the guitar, along with a pearloid fingerboard and an exquisite pickguard.

Santos Hernández Flamenco Guitar 1925

Type and body: Flamenco acoustic guitar. Spruce top. Cypress back and sides.
Neck and Fingerboard: Mahogany neck. Ebony fingerboard.

The late nineteenth century was when the lines, the shapes, and, most important, the sounds of the Spanish classical guitar would be settled. Antonio de Torres Jurado, the greatest luthier of the time, established the standard. The next generation of outstanding makers—the Ramírez brothers in Madrid and Enrique Garcia in Barcelona—took the form established by Torres and made it even better.

As great as the guitars from these masters were, they had a built-in problem. Made from the finest tone woods, with exquisite and painstaking attention to detail, they sounded beautiful but cost a small fortune. They had become refined. This left the flamenco players, the *tacaores*, grasping for a less expensive guitar that would suit their needs, one that would have the brightness, the volume, the percussive attack to accompany the best flamenco singers and dancers in whatever environment they wanted to perform.

Santos Hernández was a master luthier who learned his craft under Manuel Ramírez in Madrid. So good was Hernández that before the great virtuoso Andrés Segovia moved to a Hauser guitar, he used a Hernández guitar for the first twenty-five years of his brilliant career. And just as his master, Ramírez, understood the special needs of flamenco players, Hernández took the form of the flamenco guitar to the highest level, equal to the best Spanish classical guitars.

The key to defining the flamenco guitar was in the choice of the woods. They needed to be abundant and inexpensive but capable of standing up to years of use and abuse. Cypress was the choice for the back and sides, greatly reducing a major cost factor in the building of the guitar. Cypress is lighter than either mahogany or rosewood and has a hardness that contributes to the attacking sound of the flamenco guitar. Spruce was still used for the top, as it was from the time of Stradivari and continues to be in the great majority of acoustic guitars. Mahogany was used for the neck and the fingerboard was ebony. By mixing valuable tone woods with less expensive lumber, Hernández found the ideal combination of quality and price to make a perfect flamenco guitar.

It was not just a matter of wood. Hernández was a brilliant maker who understood duende, that ineffable feeling of flamenco spirit, and, along with his compatriot Domingo Esteso, defined the shape, style, and sound of the flamenco guitar for the rest of the twentieth century.

Domingo Esteso Flamenco Guitar 1926

Type and body: Flamenco acoustic guitar.
Spruce top. Cypress back and sides.
Neck and Fingerboard: Mahogany neck.
Rosewood fingerboard.

Although the classical guitar and the flamenco guitar look alike and have evolved from the same DNA, the two guitars are quite different. The flamenco guitar serves the music and dancing of the art of flamenco. It must accompany a singer or dancer, or both. It is required, on occasion, to be a soloist. It must be heard above the unique rhythms and sounds of *palmas altas,* the percussive clapping so central to flamenco, and the zapateado, the unique tap dancing that is at flamenco's heart. The guitar must have duende, a soulful force, heartbreakingly soft in tone and volume at one moment and startlingly bright and loud the next.

The beginning of the change in the two distinct styles of guitar can be traced to the great Spanish luthiers of the nineteenth century: the Ramírez brothers and Antonio de Torres Jurado. And perhaps back even further to the great Pagés brothers in Andalucia, the birthplace of flamenco.

As the fan brace was established as the best way to secure the top of the guitar against the tension of the strings, so classical Spanish guitar music grew exponentially, which was helped, of course, by the emergence of the great Spanish composers of the time, led by Fernando Sor. This, in turn, led to better, stronger, more beautiful instruments that were made with the finest woods, refined in tone and sustain, and expensive—well beyond the reach of ordinary guitarists.

As classical music grew in popularity throughout Spain in the nineteenth century, so flamenco grew in popularity in Andalucia in the early part of the twentieth century. Domingo Esteso had learned his craft under Manuel Ramírez in Madrid, and after his master's death, he established his own workshop in 1917. Esteso pioneered the development of the modern flamenco guitar, exquisitely built but lighter, brighter, louder—and less expensive—than the best classical guitars.

Born in the late nineteenth century, virtuoso guitarist Ramón Montoya straddled this period of transition between the differing styles of Spanish guitar. He was the greatest flamenco guitarist of his time, and it was natural that he would want the best guitar available, in this case one from the hand of Domingo Esteso. Montoya was not simply a guitarist. His collaboration with the best singers and dancers led to enormous advances in flamenco music and dance, including the creation of new dances, including the farruca.

Gibson
L-5
1928

Type and body: Archtop acoustic guitar.
Spruce top. Maple back and sides.
Neck and Fingerboard: Mahogany and maple
neck. Ebony fingerboard.

It is hard to overstate the importance of May-belle Carter and her Gibson L-5 in the history of American music. With her brother-in-law A. P. Carter (brother to Maybelle's husband, Ezra) and A. P.'s wife, Sara (who was Maybelle's cousin), they formed the Carter Family, the first successful country music group, whose influence on virtually every genre of American music would be profound.

Maybelle's deceptively simple finger style, in which she played a melody with her thumb on the bass strings and strummed the chords on the upper strings, became known as the Carter Scratch. A generation of 1960s folk singers used the Carter Scratch as their basic guitar technique. But it was the idea of articulating a melody on a guitar that made Maybelle such an influence on country, blue-grass, folk, pop, and rock. She may well have been the first de facto lead guitarist in American popu-lar music. Maybelle's style became the foundation for a generation of guitarists after her, not just for her particular technique but for how her combina-tion of bass and strum seemed to create a forceful rhythmic pulse in Carter Family songs.

Just as Orville Gibson created the archtop guitar by carving the top of the guitar from one piece of wood, so the great Gibson designer Lloyd Loar took the archtop to the next level with his L-5, which debuted in 1922, and has been in produc-tion, with many variations, ever since. The L-5 is now regarded as one of the most important guitar designs of all time. Among Loar's innovations were the two f-holes on his archtops, features of violin design, that replaced the single oval sound hole on Gibson's original Style O archtop. Loar's design for the L-5, with its tap-tuned top, was the basis for all the subsequent Gibson archtops and included an adjustable bridge and an adjustable truss rod, by which the angle of the guitar's neck, and, therefore, the action of the guitar, could be adjusted to suit the player.

Maybelle, who would eventually be known as Mother Maybelle, had a long and influential career in country music, and her recordings are consid-ered to be seminal. Listen to "Can the Circle be Unbroken," "Bury Me under the Weeping Willow," and especially "Wildwood Flower" to get a full sense of Maybelle's unique guitar style and the Carter Family's place in American popular music.

The Carter Family, c.1931. Left to right: Maybelle Carter with her glorious L-5, her cousin Sara Carter, and A. P. Carter.

Guitars

Stella Twelve-String 1928

Type and body: Twelve-string acoustic guitar. Spruce top. Mahogany back and sides.
Neck and Fingerboard: Mahogany neck. "Ebonized" pearwood fingerboard.

The two twelve-string acoustic guitars featured in this book (see also pages 90–91) could not be more different, even if they were made in the same era. While the guitar of the great Mexican-American singer Lydia Mendoza was made in the grand Mexican style, the Stella twelve-string played by Huddie Ledbetter (better known as Lead Belly) was made in the Italian style of lutherie common in and around New York and New Jersey.

Stella guitars were made by Italian luthiers at the Oscar Schmidt Company in Jersey City, just across the Hudson River from Manhattan. Factory superintendent Rocco Carlucci, a luthier of great skill, almost certainly supervised the design and building of Stella guitars. Although inexpensive for their time, and sold in huge numbers through mail order, Stella guitars are considered among the best-made guitars of the first half of the twentieth century. Just as with other budget brands, including Kay and Silvertone, interest in Stellas has increased in recent years, not least because noted players, including Kurt Cobain, played vintage Stella guitars.

The twelve-string Stella played by Lead Belly is among the most famous Stella guitars of all. Lead Belly bought the guitar new from Stella in 1939, a date that suggests that this was one of the last guitars made by the Oscar Schmidt Company, because it sold the Stella brand itself in 1939. The guitar remained in the family after Lead Belly's death and is now in the collection of the National Museum of African American History and Culture in Washington, D.C.

Lead Belly had a difficult life and career, becoming famous for various incarcerations, recording while incarcerated, and finding eventual release partly because he was a recognized recording artist. Discovered in jail by folklorist and ethnomusicologist John Lomax and his son Alan, Lead Belly became known as a folk and blues singer and was an excellent guitarist. One of Lead Belly's strongest, most famous songs, "The Bourgeois Blues," recorded on his Stella, deals with an overtly racist incident Lead Belly and his wife experienced when visiting Washington, D.C., to record with Alan Lomax.

Along with this recording of the song by Lead Belly, look for a brilliant cover by Ry Cooder, from his album *Chicken Skin Music*.

A studio photograph of Lead Belly with his Stella, c.1945.

National Tricone Style 4 Resonator Guitar 1929

Type and body: German Silver acoustic resonator guitar.
Neck and Fingerboard: Mahogany neck. Ebony fingerboard.

The pursuit of more volume has been the obsession of luthiers since the time of the lute. In traditional Spanish guitars, larger bodies gave more depth and bass, but at a cost to the sweet tones of the smaller bodied guitars.

George Beauchamp was a Texas-born vaudeville performer who played the violin and the lap steel guitar, and his role in the invention of the electric guitar is only now being fully recognized. Like many performers, he wanted more volume from his guitar, and he had the idea to attach the horn of a gramophone to a guitar. In Los Angeles, Beauchamp discussed the idea with Slovak immigrant Ján Dopjera, now known as John Dopyera. With the can-do fervor that was in the air in California in the 1920s, Dopyera got to work. Already a well-known violin and banjo maker, Dopyera knew what Beauchamp was after, and he began experimenting with Beauchamp's idea of amplifying cones.

By installing three aluminum cones into a metal guitar, Dopyera could solve several problems at once. With a thin metal body, the cones could take up the load of the strings, which on wooden guitars was the job of braces under the guitar top. The metal body was lighter and easier (and cheaper) to fabricate than the intricate joinery required of a traditional wooden guitar, and, most important, the sound of the guitar, resonating through these cones, was considerably louder than a traditional acoustic guitar. The idea was an instant success. Taken up at first by lovers of the Hawaiian guitar, the resonator guitar, as it is now known, became the preferred instrument of anyone playing in public where more volume—and a new, interesting sound—was required.

Beauchamp and Dopyera, along with the latter's brother, Rudy, started the National company to build and sell "resophonic" guitars. While Beauchamp went on to work with colleague Paul Barth and Swiss inventor Adolph Rickenbacker to create an electric steel guitar, the Dopyera brothers took the tricone idea in new directions with the Dobro Manufacturing Company (DOpyera BROthers), eventually producing several models of beautifully made guitars with different variations of cone resonators and materials. National and Dobro guitars share the same DNA, even if both had individual histories since their conception.

Gibson
L-00
1931

Type and body: Acoustic guitar. Spruce top.
Mahogany back and sides.
Neck and Fingerboard: Mahogany neck.
Ebony fingerboard.

Woody Guthrie was a folk singer, but he was many more things besides. Not only did he compose one of the world's favorite campfire songs, "This Land Is Your Land," but Guthrie's influence on other singers, especially Pete Seeger and a young Bob Dylan, cannot be overstated. That he chose as his guitar the modest Gibson flattop L-00 is not out of character for a man who regarded himself as much a man of the people as a political activist.

"This Land Is Your Land," Guthrie's most famous song, was written as a riposte to the popular patriotic song "America the Beautiful." Guthrie believed the lyrics of that song were both saccharine and nationalistic. The irony is that almost a century later "This Land Is Your Land" is sung as a campfire sing-along, stripped by familiarity of its radical socialist undertones.

Guthrie had many guitars, and apparently he often gave them away. Just as well, since the L-00 was easy to give away. An inexpensive flattop parlor guitar with a shallow body, it was at the bottom of Gibson's range. Nevertheless, it could hold its own in playability and tone. Gibson never set out to make *bad* guitars; it just recognized that not everyone could afford a really good guitar. It was a clever strategy; the L-00, along with Gibson's other budget flattop models, made up more than 50 percent of its sales in the 1930s.

Ever the provocateur, Woody Guthrie put a sticker on his guitars that read, "This Machine Kills Fascists." Perhaps it's not the slogan that Gibson might have chosen, but the "machine" lives on in popular culture as an important symbol of mid-twentieth-century activism, a predictor of the protest movement of the 1960s and the music that went with it.

Woody Guthrie with his ubiquitous anti-fascist sticker on his L-00 in 1943.

Rickenbacker
Frying Pan
1931

Type and body: Hawaiian-style lap steel guitar.
Maple body (production models: aluminum).
Neck and Fingerboard: Maple neck and
fingerboard (production models: aluminum).
Pickups: Single-coil wound horseshoe magnets.

Texan vaudevillian and entrepreneur George Beauchamp had already made his mark on the guitar world with his idea of the resonating guitar (see pages 76–77), an instrument that would eventually find fame as the Dobro.

As a musician, Beauchamp was aware of the musical styles of the day. One of the biggest musical trends in the 1920s and 1930s was for Hawaiian music, where the lead instrument was a guitar held across the player's lap and played with a bar moved up and down the strings to change the pitch. As a lead instrument, the resonator guitar was much louder than the typical wooden acoustic guitar, but Beauchamp wanted something even louder.

His own experiments with an acoustic guitar taught him about feedback, that age-old problem where secondary vibrations in the wood are amplified through the pickup, creating a high-pitched howl that brings the music to a screeching halt. Beauchamp had the idea of eliminating all vibrations in the guitar by fabricating an instrument from metal that would have his basic magnetic pickup installed. Swiss immigrant

Adolph Rickenbacker fabricated the metal pieces for the early resonator guitars and was close to Beauchamp and the Dopyeras at National. So it was to Rickenbacker that Beauchamp went with his idea for a solid electrified guitar.

The result was the world's first practical electric guitar, the Rickenbacker Frying Pan, so called because the neck is attached to a pan-shaped body that is actually little more than a mount for George Beauchamp's very basic pickup.

The Rickenbacker was not held and played like a typical guitar; instead, it was placed across the player's lap in the style favored by Hawaiian guitar players. This is how the lap steel came to be known, and it is how the Rickenbacker, both as the first playable electric guitar and as a lap steel, holds its place in the pantheon of guitars.

The guitar pictured is Beauchamp's prototype for the Frying Pan.

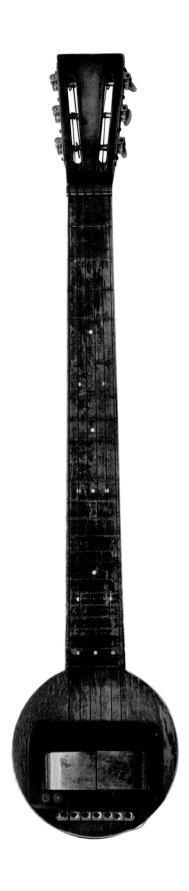

Julián Gómez Ramirez
Jazz Guitar
1932

Type and body: Two-piece flattop jazz guitar.
Rosewood back and sides.
Neck and Fingerboard: Brazilian rosewood neck.
Mahogany fingerboard.

The pursuit of more volume has driven guitar makers for as long as guitars have been made. Gibson began the modern era of acoustic guitars with their acoustic archtops, a style soon to be copied by many others, with Epiphone and Stromberg among the best.

In the age of jazz bands, whose frontline instruments were loud—with the saxophones, trumpets, and trombones of the typical jazz ensemble—it was crucially important for the guitar to be audible. Before electric guitars became standard jazz instruments, the acoustic jazz guitar was left to play the rhythm part, and the best players created beautiful sequences of complex chord shapes to complement the noise up front.

French musicians loved jazz, a sexy American musical import, and they brought to it a uniquely French flair and style, exemplified by the gypsy jazz guitarists such as Django Reinhardt and Baro Ferret. These players needed louder guitars, and the best luthiers in France were eager to meet the demand of modern jazz players.

Trained as a maker of Spanish guitars in the Ramírez workshop in Madrid, Julián Gómez Ramirez set up shop in Paris and took his luthier skills in a new direction with this large, steel-stringed jazz guitar. To make it strong enough to hold the tension of the steel strings, Ramirez anchored them directly to the guitar's tail. The headstock is typical of a classical guitar, but it is the body that shows Ramirez's bravura design skills. The large body produced a big sound, and the two large Art Deco lunette sound holes in the upper body of the guitar delivered that sound. The neck is short scale, joining the body at the twelfth fret, typical of a Spanish or parlor guitar. Ramirez extended the fingerboard by ten frets and created a large, scalloped cutaway to accommodate the player's hands. Ramirez, with his sure design skills, gave his guitar an Art Deco symmetry with a double cutaway. Baro Ferret used this guitar on the many recordings he made with his friend Django Reinhardt.

National Style O 1933

Type and body: Acoustic resonator guitar.
Pressed and nickel-plated brass body.
Neck and Fingerboard: Maple neck. "Ebonized"
maple fingerboard.

Vaudevillian, innovator, and entrepreneur George Beauchamp had already established National as the most important maker of resonator guitars when, for reasons that are lost to history, he fell out with his partner, John Dopyera, and his brothers. And although Dopyera kept his investment in National, the brothers went on to found Dobro (DOpyera BROthers) and make their own instruments based on a single-cone resonator.

Undaunted by the breakup, Beauchamp forged ahead with his single-cone resonator guitar instead of the three cones in the group's original tricone model. This new guitar was again aimed at the market for players of Hawaiian music, with its distinctive portamento swoops and slides, created by using steel bars to change the notes of the strings. With a single cone mounted in the center of the guitar's lower body, the bridge is attached to the cone and hovers over the strings, the so-called "biscuit bridge" design. Two f-holes punctuate either side of the guitar's upper body, and the metalwork is beautifully etched with palm trees, evocative of Hawaii and aimed at the guitar's target audience of Hawaiian music fans.

The guitar also found a base among blues players, who liked the louder volume of the National, and it was sold at a cheaper price than most wooden guitars of the time. Robert Johnson and Son House both recorded on single-cone National guitars, and these recordings are recognized as some of the most important ever made. Half a century later, Mark Knopfler of Dire Straits used his National Style O on his song "Romeo and Juliet." Whereas the blues players played with a slide, or in Son House's case a length of copper tube slid over one of his fingers, Knopfler plays it as a conventional guitar. His opening arpeggio on "Romeo and Juliet" is famous, as is the rest of his playing on the song. The guitar itself was featured on the cover of the 1985 Dire Straits album *Brothers in Arms*, which prompted renewed interest in resonator guitars among collectors and musicians alike.

Guitars

Selmer Maccaferri #271 1933

Type and body: Flattop jazz guitar. Spruce top. Indian rosewood back and sides.
Neck and Fingerboard: Walnut neck. Ebony fingerboard.

France's obsession with jazz in the early and mid-twentieth century was in great part due to two people: Josephine Baker and Django Reinhardt (and his band). A part of the allure of jazz for French music fans was an early sense of outsiderness. For centuries, chanson, an ephemeral term meaning a French song of virtually any era, had held sway throughout the country. As France emerged from the ravages of World War I, traditional French songs didn't seem to fit the new mood. Jazz, ushered in with naughty verve by Josephine Baker in the 1920s, fit the times perfectly, and musicians rushed to play this new, free, but technically demanding music. The best of these great players were Django Reinhardt and violinist Stéphane Grappelli, along with the Ferret brothers. The Quintette du Hot Club de France was a supergroup in which Reinhardt and Grappelli played.

Founded in the nineteenth century, Selmer is a producer of high-end wind instruments, but early in the jazz era, it saw an opportunity to make jazz guitars for these new musicians. The trouble was, it did not make guitars. For this, Selmer turned to Mario Maccaferri, a guitarist, inventor, luthier, and entrepreneur, who provided both the expertise and the design for this guitar.

Maccaferri's design brilliance is everywhere in this guitar: the squat shape of the body; the elegant single cutaway, allowing the player's left hand to reach the higher frets; the tailpiece, which looks like a detail from the Chrysler building; and the signature move, the Art Deco D-shaped sound hole. The principal technical innovations include the use of a truss rod, a long steel bar that reinforces the neck to let it take the tension off the steel strings, and a detachable resonator inside the guitar to add volume, an innovation that was dropped after Maccaferri left the company. It was not the only change. Selmer also reduced the sound hole to a small, and equally beautiful, oval.

After playing Julián Gómez Ramirez, Stromberg, and Levin guitars, Django Reinhardt settled on the Selmer Maccaferri for his recording and playing career, an endorsement that cemented the success of Maccaferri's design and continues to make the guitar highly desirable today.

After his success with Selmer, Mario Maccaferri moved to New York, where he opened a plastics factory to produce, among other things, clothespins, a plastic reed for woodwinds that is still in production, a plastic guitar, and a plastic ukulele, which was a huge success, selling in the millions.

Acosta Twelve-string 1935

Type and body: Twelve-string acoustic guitar. Spruce top. Mahogany back and sides.
Neck and Fingerboard: Mahogany neck. Ebony fingerboard.

The twelve-string acoustic guitar is a gentle giant, a throwback to the earliest days of multicourse guitars, whose courses, or pairs of strings, could be tuned in unison or in octaves or in any other way the player desired. The typical twelve-string has six courses of double strings tuned with the four lower courses in octaves and the two upper courses in unison.

Twelve-strings have never really caught on with the guitar-buying public, even if the twelve-string guitar has had some famous players. Because of the extra tension placed on the neck and the bridge by having twelve strings in tension, and a large headstock to accommodate twelve tuners, the twelve-string has to be strong and is, therefore, big and heavy. On the electric side, Roger McGuinn and George Harrison with their Rickenbackers, and Jimmy Page with his famous double-neck Gibson EDS-1275, certainly made an impact. For Page, he couldn't play "Stairway to Heaven" without a twelve-string for the long intro, and the Gibson fit the bill perfectly, even if its use was limited. The sound of an acoustic twelve-string guitar is unique, almost as if a chorus of strings were creating a warm and harmonic sound.

Lydia Mendoza was the best-known Mexican-American performer of her time, whose work helped establish Tejano music as a truly American art form. Wisconsin-based luthier and musicologist Todd Cambio has done more than anyone to bring to light the maker of Mendoza's famous twelve-string. Mendoza's guitar was made in San Antonio, Texas, by Guadalupe Acosta, a Tejano luthier of great artistry. Acosta's work was among the best of the celebrated style of Mexican string instrument making, and Mendoza's twelve-string guitar is a perfect example of Mexican instrument style. Although the Acosta family believes that walnut was sometimes used on the bodies of its better guitars, Lydia's twelve-string has a spruce top and mahogany back and sides. It features two geometric lunette shapes in the upper body that suggest a lightness in what was, without doubt, a heavy guitar. The Acosta family has had a long tradition of instrument making in San Antonio, and many of their guitars are still being played today.

Tejano singer and guitarist Mendoza deserves a place in the pantheon of guitar greats for a body of recordings that often featured her spectacular guitar playing. Although she was born in Houston, Texas, in 1916 and spoke English, Mendoza only performed in Spanish. She had a long and successful career, including a hit single, "Mal Hombre," which was also the title of a CD issued during the 1990s. Look for Lydia's recording of "Palida Luna," recorded in El Paso, Texas, in 1935. The syncopation in her guitar playing echoes the complex rhythms of the polkas that were a foundation stone of Texas swing.

Lydia Mendoza with her twelve-string, c.1937.

Martin
D-28
1935

Type and body: Flattop Dreadnought acoustic
guitar. Spruce top. Rosewood back and sides.
Neck and Fingerboard: Mahogany neck.
Ebony fingerboard.

Sometimes it is just impossible to separate a
great guitar from those who played it. With early
Martins, it could be Elvis Presley's 1935 Martin
D-18, bought by him on an installment plan. When
he was finally able to take it home, Elvis asked the
store owner to put his name on the top in goofy
stick-on letters. No matter, that D-18 remains one
of the greatest ever made or played. Then there is
the 1941 D-28 owned and played by Hank Williams,
which is now owned and played by Neil Young.
According to Young, it is the guitar played by
Williams on his last gig at the Grand Ole Opry, that
weekly institution of Nashville country music.

As undoubtedly great as those guitars are, the runaway winner is this D-28—for its provenance; for
the indignities it has suffered and survived, including the enlargement of its sound hole; and, above all,
for the music that has been created and played on it.
This majestic Martin D-28 has to be considered one
of the outstanding treasures of the American guitar.

First designed in 1916 but sold under another
name, the large Dreadnought was reestablished

in the Martin line in 1931 and quickly became the
six-string acoustic guitar against which all others
were judged. The Martin factory gave this instrument the number 58957, and it was, from the
start, a swanky guitar. With an Adirondack spruce
top, characteristic herringbone binding, and
Brazilian rosewood sides and back, this was the
top of the line of acoustic guitars and soon became
a mainstay of folk music and bluegrass.

From new, it went on a circuitous, unknown journey until it was found with no strings, and looking
badly beaten, by a young Clarence White in a guitar
shop in Los Angeles in 1959. White and his brother
brought the guitar back to life, and with this guitar,
White came to define the acoustic guitar as a solo
bluegrass instrument.

Tony Rice acquired the guitar in 1975, when it was
in a virtually unplayable condition. With the expertise of several luthiers, Rice brought the forty-
year-old Herringbone, as D-28s are nicknamed,
back to life. From then it became an intrinsic part
of Rice's brilliant flat-picking bluegrass style,
almost as if this guitar were destined to be at the
center of bluegrass music for almost its entire life.

Look for Rice playing the bluegrass classic "Nine
Pound Hammer" at a bluegrass festival with his
all-star band, and be astonished at the sweet sound
of the guitar, and Rice's virtuoso playing.

Tony Rice with his priceless D-28 slung over his
shoulder, 1999.

Epiphone Emperor 1936

Type and body: Archtop acoustic guitar.
Spruce top. Maple back and sides.
Neck and Fingerboard: Walnut and maple neck.
Ebony fingerboard.

The 1930s was the high point of big band swing and jazz, and the best guitars of this period—the D'Angelico New Yorker, the Gibson ES-150, the Stromberg G-1, the Levin Deluxe, and this Epiphone Emperor—were aimed squarely at professional jazz players.

The Emperor is not just a gorgeous guitar; it is a huge guitar, with an 18½-inch (47-cm) lower body and a long neck. Like the Levin and the D'Angelico, it was a luxury carved spruce guitar with a large, floating, tortoiseshell pickguard (with a shape similar to the Levin), with curly maple back and sides and gold-plated tuners.

The company that would become Epiphone was founded in New York City by Greek immigrant Anastasios Stathopoulo in 1903. On the death of Anastasios in 1915, his son Epaminondas, known to all as Epi, took over the business, focusing on banjos and guitars and becoming Epiphone in 1928. From that moment on, Epi Stathopoulo built the business into a giant of guitar- and banjo-making, eventually focusing solely on guitars.

The Epiphone Emperor was a jazz guitar, and the best-known player of the Emperor was rhythm guitarist Freddie Green of the Count Basie Orchestra. The guitar really was a rhythm instrument in jazz at that time, and Green was the best rhythm player of them all. John Lennon, another great Epiphone player, later said, speaking of his time in the Beatles, that he could drive the band. It was clear that Freddie Green could drive a band, too, even if—as a rhythm guitarist—his role was to be in the background. In a sublime fourteen-minute live version of "Honeysuckle Rose" recorded at Carnegie Hall in 1938, Freddie Green can be heard taking a rhythm solo while playing for Benny Goodman's ensemble.

In apparent acknowledgment that the Emperor needed to be a solo instrument, Epiphone created the Soloist Emperor, with a single cutaway that allowed for the player to reach all the way to the twentieth fret.

Acquired by its main rival, Gibson, in 1957, Epiphone is still making guitars, both as lower-cost versions of well-known Gibson guitars and continuing its own lines.

Gibson ES-150 1936

Type and body: Archtop electric guitar. Spruce top. Maple back and sides.
Neck and Fingerboard: Mahogany neck. Rosewood fingerboard.
Pickups: Single-blade Charlie Christian pickup.

There is a moment in jazz when the music changed from instrumental versions of standard songs and show tunes—the so-called Great American Songbook—into specially composed tunes for a jazz ensemble. This moment might have been invented for guitar virtuoso Charlie Christian, who, despite his tragically short life, left an indelible mark on American popular music, playing in Benny Goodman's ensembles. Unveiled in 1936, and purchased by Charlie Christian that same year, the Gibson ES-150 was the first electric archtop offered by Gibson. From that moment, popular music would never sound the same again.

First, the name: ES stands for "electric Spanish," which is a little odd, since the Gibson archtop, with its distinctive f-holes, its floating pickguard, and its Gibson sunburst, doesn't look at all Spanish, at least not in the style of a classical Spanish guitar. The number 150 represents the price of the guitar: $150. In 1936, this was not exactly cheap, but it did come with an amplifier, a cord, and a case. For professional musicians looking to move from purely acoustic guitars into something that could be heard in front of a blazing horn section, it was the perfect solution, and arrived at exactly the right time.

The guitar was beautifully made, with a carved spruce top (the archtop), maple back and sides, and a truss rod that allowed for adjusting the neck, which would be important for both playability and tuning. But the key to the guitar's success was the pickup, a simple bar pickup mounted close to the neck. This gave the guitar a warm, mellow sound, perfect for jazz. Success was instant, especially with Charlie Christian's endorsement. Even the pickup came to be known as the "Charlie Christian pickup" and was such a triumph that Gibson continued its development as the P90, which has been widely copied and is still in production today.

Charlie Christian was one of several guitarists who moved the guitar from a band's rhythm section into the solo position. Christian's style was fluid, intensely musical, and seemingly effortless all at the same time. Jazz commentators claim Christian as an early bebop innovator. Still others believe him to be the first true rock guitarist. These claims may be fanciful, but what is irrefutable is the greatness of Christian's music and playing, mercifully preserved. Listen to the Columbia album *Solo Flight: The Genius of Charlie Christian*, and be astonished.

Gibson L-1 c.1937

Type and body: Acoustic guitar. Sitka spruce top. Mahogany back and sides.
Neck and Fingerboard: Mahogany neck. Rosewood fingerboard.

Robert Johnson is generally regarded as the greatest blues singer and guitarist of the early part of the twentieth century. And although myths about his life abound, including the Faustian pact he is said to have made with the devil, little about his life is actually known.

What survives are the twenty-nine recordings and twelve alternative takes that Johnson recorded over two sessions in San Antonio and Dallas, Texas, in 1936 and 1937. Some of the most treasured blues standards come from those sessions, including "Crossroad Blues," with Johnson apparently burnishing his devil myth in the lyrics, and "Sweet Home Chicago."

Only three pictures of Johnson are known to have survived, including this studio photograph, in which Johnson appears impeccably dressed from his jaunty hat right down to his highly polished brogues. The guitar he holds, and there is no evidence that it was actually Johnson's own, is a Gibson L-1 from 1937. Were it actually his, the Gibson L-1 would be an appropriate instrument for Johnson to own and play. A flattop acoustic that had started life as an archtop, the L-1—introduced in 1926—satisfied a growing demand for inexpensive flattop acoustic guitars at a then relatively modest price of fifty dollars. In this photograph, the date of which suggests it might have been taken for marketing his records, Johnson is shown forming a bar chord on the fifth fret, a simple gesture that nevertheless indicates Johnson's easy ability as a guitarist. And it is Johnson's musicianship, as well as his plaintive Delta tenor, that caught the attention of blues lovers and record buyers everywhere.

In 1938, a year after this photograph was taken, Johnson died of unknown causes at the tragically young age of twenty-seven.

So little is known about Robert Johnson that this studio photograph of him is a treasure.

Hermann Hauser Guitar 1937

Type and body: Classical guitar. Spruce top. Brazilian rosewood back and sides.
Neck and Fingerboard: Mahogany neck. Ebony fingerboard.

An intriguing link between classical guitars and modern American acoustic guitars is that the maker of this instrument, Hermann Hauser, was greatly influenced, at least in his early years, by the work of Johann Georg Stauffer. Stauffer, in turn, mentored Christian Frederick Martin, founder of C. F. Martin & Company. It was those smaller, slight-bodied Viennese-style instruments that would be the genesis of American acoustic guitars. And they were the guitars that Hauser both made and played early in his career.

In 1913 Hauser met Catalan virtuoso Miguel Llobet, who was on tour in Munich. Llobet was playing his Torres guitar, which at that time represented the best of Spanish guitar design. Hauser was intrigued by the Torres and studied it closely. From that moment on, Hauser dedicated himself to making better and better instruments in the Torres style.

Andrés Segovia was an emerging guitar virtuoso, playing a Torres, naturally, when he met Hauser, reportedly, courtesy of his fellow countryman Llobet. Segovia acquired his first Hauser in the late 1920s and played it for several years. In 1937 Segovia acquired this guitar, which he described in a now-famous quote to be "the greatest guitar of our epoch." Segovia became the greatest virtuoso of the mid-twentieth century, and it was his playing that brought attention both to the repertoire of classical guitar and the instruments themselves.

With a top made of two pieces of spruce and Brazilian rosewood back and sides, the Hauser design is the ultimate expression of the Spanish style of Ramírez and Torres—loud, balanced, and bright, with a beautiful sustain. This guitar is now in the collection of the Metropolitan Museum of Art in New York, whose curator of musical instruments, Jayson Dobney, is a relentless champion of the best guitar making, old and new.

Gibson
SJ-200
1938

Type and body: "Jumbo" acoustic guitar.
Spruce top. Rosewood back and sides.
Neck and Fingerboard: Maple neck. Ebony
fingerboard.

You could say that that Royal Navy started it all when it launched HMS *Dreadnought* in 1906. The biggest, baddest battleship ever built, it started a naval arms race unlike anything that had ever been seen, and it immediately became embedded in the public imagination. When Martin introduced their new, extra-large guitar in 1916 (but not under their own name), they naturally called it a Dreadnought. Buoyed by the success of these big guitars made for the Oliver Ditson Company, Martin introduced the Dreadnought in 1931 under the Martin name. The competition took notice. If extra-large was what the public wanted, extra-large the public would get.

Gibson responded in 1937 with its extra-large Super Jumbo guitar that, like Martin's Dreadnought, was a loud, lush, resonant flattop with a big bass tone. By 1939, the name had changed to SJ-200, but the guitar itself was unchanged, with a very large 16⅞-inch (43-cm) body and beautiful details, including a red spruce top, rosewood back and sides, a characteristic Gibson sunburst finish, and the most extravagantly decorated pickguard

on the market. The SJ-200 was a runaway success for Gibson, and the guitar has remained in production, with various changes to details and materials, from that day until now.

The Reverend Gary Davis was born into virtual poverty in Laurens, South Carolina, in 1898 and had a harsh upbringing. His mother abandoned him, and his father was reputedly shot dead by a sheriff in Birmingham, Alabama. Gary, blind from a young age, was left to be raised by his grandmother. As he grew up, Gary became a Christian minister and moved first to North Carolina and then to New York, where he eventually became quite famous in the early folk and blues circuits. His songs were covered by, among others, Bob Dylan and Peter, Paul and Mary. Look for a stunning 1967 recording that shows Gary, a large man, singing with a plaintive blues voice and playing his big Gibson SJ-200 with a unique two-finger guitar technique.

Levin
Orkestergitarr De Luxe
1938

Type and body: Archtop guitar. Spruce top.
Maple back and sides.
Neck and Fingerboard: Maple neck. Mahogany
fingerboard.

Levin guitars may be the best instruments nobody has ever heard of, but over the course of its eighty-year history, this Swedish company produced more than half a million instruments, including mandolins, flattops, banjos, and even lutes.

At the end of the nineteenth century, woodworker and entrepreneur Herman Carlson Levin went to New York to find work as a carpenter. Instead, he got a job making guitars and decided to return to Gothenburg, Sweden, to open a guitar factory. Levin's timing was perfect; the market for guitars was booming, and soon the factory was turning out a range of instruments, all of excellent quality. The 1920s and 1930s saw an unprecedented boom in jazz and swing, and every band needed a guitarist for rhythm and occasional solos. Levin's "orchestra guitar" was designed in 1937 to fill this niche.

With an extravagantly carved headstock; carved spruce top and maple back and sides; a large, beautifully shaped pickguard; and gold-plated tuners, the Orkestergitarr was truly an expensive, deluxe,

top-of-the-line guitar. Fred Guy, Duke Ellington's longtime guitarist, bought a Levin Orkestergitarr De Luxe while on tour in Sweden in 1938, and Guy famously lent his guitar to Django Reinhardt to play when Reinhardt toured the United States with Ellington in 1946. These endorsements didn't translate into large sales and this glorious Levin guitar is all but forgotten today.

Perhaps it was its location in Gothenburg, on the southwest coast of Sweden, that made it difficult for the Levin guitar factory to survive. It certainly was not a problem with quality. So good were these guitars that, for a period of twenty years, Levin successfully sold guitars under the Goya name in the United States. Even Julie Andrews played a Goya guitar in *The Sound of Music*. But "Doh, a deer, a female deer" was not enough to save the company. A series of bad business deals undermined the Goya brand, and, by the time the Levin business was taken over by Martin in 1973, dwindling interest in its own brand all but cemented the company's failure.

Les Paul
The Log
1941

Type and body: ProtoType semi-hollow-body electric guitar. Solid pine four-by-four. Epiphone acoustic body parts.
Neck and Fingerboard: Gibson mahogany neck. Rosewood fingerboard.
Pickups: Two Les Paul homemade pickups.

It is hard to describe how brilliant a musician, and how inventive a technologist, Les Paul was. First, Les Paul was the most famous guitarist in North America, and he was smart and adaptable, easily switching from country to jazz to his lightweight pop. With his wife, Mary Ford, he had hit after hit with his own radio and television shows and major concert performances. He toured extensively, and for the last fifteen years of his life, he had a weekly gig at the Iridium club on New York's Upper West Side, which he played right up until his death in 2009 at the age of ninety-four.

However, it is with this odd-looking guitar that Les Paul made his indelible mark on popular music and pop culture. Early electric guitars were principally archtops with pickups attached, and they suffered terribly from feedback—that high-frequency squeal caused by sound waves from the amplifier speakers creating further vibrations in the guitar, which fed back into the pickup and then the amplifier. Paul thought that he could eliminate this feedback if, instead of mounting the pickup on the top of a hollow guitar,

he could attach it to a solid piece of wood, which would then attach to the guitar's neck. Paul went to the Epiphone factory in Long Island City in New York and got to work. Using a four-by-four plank, Paul attached his own homemade pickups and a spare Gibson neck, strung it up, plugged it in, and sure enough, the feedback was eliminated. He sawed an Epiphone archtop body in half to attach to the four-by-four, and the result was the Log, which he started playing in concerts and on the radio. He famously brought the idea to Gibson, who weren't interested. They were having too much success with their existing lines of flattops and archtops.

Enter Leo Fender, who was developing a solid-body guitar that would become the Telecaster in 1950. Gibson, realizing they were about to be trumped by upstart rivals, and working on their own versions of a solid-body guitar, called Les Paul and asked him to come to the factory in Kalamazoo, Michigan, to advise on their new range of electric guitars. The result of that meeting was an endorsement deal for the Gibson Les Paul, a guitar that is still in production today.

It is impossible to overstate the impact Les Paul has had on popular music, and music technology, in the twentieth century. Among his hits, listen to "How High the Moon" and "Mockingbird Hill," and marvel at his effortless, self-taught musicianship.

D'Angelico Guitars
New Yorker
1943

Type and body: Archtop acoustic guitar.
Spruce top. Maple back and sides.
Neck and Fingerboard: Maple neck.
Ebony fingerboard.

No story of guitar design would be complete without the great Italian instrument makers going back to Stradivari, the luthier from Cremona, Italy, whose violins are still played and celebrated every day somewhere in the world. It was inevitable once these expert craftsmen arrived in the United States that they would have a profound influence on American guitar design. And that is exactly what happened, especially with two New York makers: John D'Angelico and his protégé, Jimmy D'Aquisto.

D'Angelico was born in New York City into a family steeped in the luthier tradition. Young D'Angelico learned his craft with a relative, Raphael Ciani, who made violins and bowlback mandolins, a classic Italian type. D'Angelico began his own business very simply by copying the Gibson L-5, Lloyd Loar's great f-hole arch-top, designed in 1922, and a standard-bearer that is still in production. But D'Angelico took the L-5 design and made it his own. Everything about the guitar said "New York," from the reference to skyscrapers in the "rising steps" shape on the pickguard and the tailpiece to D'Angelico's name emblazoned on the headstock with "New York" just below.

Other style cues are a mixture of old Italy and the New World. Italian mandolins often had extravagantly carved headstocks, a feature reworked enthusiastically by Gibson with their mandolins. D'Angelico took this idea and ran with it, creating highly carved and ornamented headstocks. He further adorned the headstock with inlays and adornments that could have been lifted straight from the exterior of the 1930 Chrysler building, the pinnacle of American Art Deco design.

Although manufacturing standards were said to be variable, this did not stop the best players, especially in New York City, from wanting D'Angelico's guitars. By the time of his death at the age of fifty-nine, D'Angelico had produced 1,164 guitars, the last ten of them completed by D'Aquisto. This is a relatively small output of outstanding guitars from one of the greatest luthiers of all time.

Guitars

Paul Bigsby
#2
1948

Type and body: Single-cutaway, solid-body electric guitar. Maple body.
Neck and Fingerboard: Maple neck through body. Rosewood fingerboard.
Pickups: One single-coil pickup.

Motorcycle racer, design engineer, inventor, and entrepreneur Paul Bigsby's legend is secure in not one but two different facets of American popular culture. First, with his friend and racing buddy Al Crocker, Bigsby designed much of the engine on the Crocker, now considered to be one of the most beautiful motorcycles ever made. Crocker racing singles and luxurious V-twins, built in Los Angeles in the early 1930s, are now among the rarest and most collectible of all antique motorcycles, bought and sold for small fortunes.

Had Paul Bigsby stuck with motorcycle design, his legacy would already have been set. It is not known when Bigsby first met either Leo Fender or Merle Travis, but what is certain is that both men had a profound influence on the course of Bigsby's life, and the design of the solid-body electric guitar.

Guitarist Merle Travis was familiar with Bigsby through Crocker motorcycles. Travis was having trouble keeping his Gibson in tune, and he took it to Bigsby to see if there might be an engineering fix to the problem. The resulting "fix" was an

entirely new tailpiece, one that not only anchored the strings effectively but had a movable bar that could change the pitch of all the strings. This was the Bigsby vibrato tailpiece, often called a whammy bar or simply a Bigsby. This device is still in production and is arguably the most important mechanical innovation on the modern electric guitar.

Impressed by Bigsby's engineering ability, in 1947 Merle Travis asked him if he could make him a guitar based on some sketches that Travis had made. The result was a solid-body electric guitar with a single cutaway that looks as if it could have been made in the early twenty-first century. Bigsby continued making beautiful and expensive custom solid-body guitars for several years, and his work became quite famous, particularly in and around Los Angeles.

Bigsby was friends with electronic engineer Leo Fender, whose radio repair shop was in Fullerton, California, just an hour down the dusty highway from Bigsby's workshop on Venice Boulevard. There is no question that Fender knew Bigsby's guitars well. The Merle Travis guitar from 1947 has design cues and solutions, especially in the flamboyant headstock, that point to Fender's own guitar designs, which would emerge, completely formed, just a couple of years later.

Fender Broadcaster 1950

Type and body: Solid-body electric guitar. Ash body.
Neck and Fingerboard: Maple neck and fingerboard.
Pickups: Two single-coil pickups.

By the late 1940s, electric guitars were in demand, even if weren't readily available. Rickenbacker had proved the concept of a guitar with a pickup. Gibson had taken the concept several steps forward with their electric archtop, and Les Paul had created his Log. Steel guitars, both held on the lap and placed on a little stand, were selling well. Paul Bigsby was becoming famous by bringing his engineering genius to the design of the solid-body electric guitar, with beautiful and forward-looking custom instruments for the famous and the wealthy, most notably a design for Merle Travis, one of the greatest guitarists in the country.

Leo Fender's expertise in electronics had already helped him design pickups for his line of steel guitars, but he and his colleagues knew that there was a nascent market for an affordable electrified guitar that could be played in a band, or at least above the sound of the drummer. As the business of steel guitars and amps grew, Leo devoted more and more energy to designing an electric guitar for mass production that could be built simply, from factory-made parts.

In Fullerton, California, Fender and his colleagues knew Bigsby, whose workshop was just up the road in downtown Los Angeles, and it is well documented that the people at Fender regarded Bigsby as the granddaddy of the solid-body guitar. So it should be no surprise that Fender looked to Bigsby's innovations as he developed the design that would be his first production guitar. Among them was the idea of placing all six tuners on the side of the headstock, and possibly the single cutaway, which allowed for guitarists to play the upper, formerly inaccessible, frets. This is not to say that Fender copied Bigsby's design, but simply that Fender recognized a good idea when he saw one.

Fender's first solid-body guitar design was the Esquire, with one pickup, of which a few were made and shown to the trade. A model with a black pickguard and two pickups was released, called the Broadcaster. The problem with using the name Broadcaster was that, on the other coast, in New York, Gretsch was using the name on its drums, and it issued a cease-and-desist letter to Fender. Leo Fender had the decals already printed, so ever

Guitars

practical, he simply cut the word *Broadcaster* off the stickers and sent them to customers with just the Fender name on the headstock. These guitars are now known as No-casters and are treasures. Changing the name to Telecaster, Fender relaunched his new two-pickup solid-body guitar in 1951. It is no exaggeration to say that the Telecaster changed the course of popular music. Such is its success that it is still in production today.

Gibson
Les Paul Gold Top
1952

Type and body: Single-cutaway, solid-body electric guitar. Mahogany body. Maple top.
Neck and Fingerboard: Mahogany neck. Rosewood fingerboard.
Pickups: Two P-90 single-coil pickups.

Throughout the 1940s Gibson was having considerable success with its archtops, including its Electric Spanish models, most notably the L-5CES (Cutaway, Electric, Spanish). Gibson was even developing a solid-body guitar, a design that, as we have seen, had already been brought to market by Rickenbacker, Paul Bigsby, and then Fender with its Telecaster.

Les Paul had tinkered away at the Epiphone factory in New York, creating his own electric solid-body guitar, the Log, and variations of the design that Paul called his Clunkers. And he had showed them to Gibson in the hopes that they might pick up some of his ideas, only to be shown the door by Gibson's senior executives. By the end of the 1940s, however, Les Paul was no longer a tinkerer, begging weekend time at Epiphone's New York factory. In fact, he was the most famous, most successful, most popular guitar player in the United States.

The story is well-known, and it was not entirely unsurprising that in 1951, responding to Fender's success with its Telecaster, visionary Gibson

CEO Ted McCarty invited Paul to look at what Gibson's designers had been doing. It was a solid-body guitar with two pickups and a cutaway, and a carved top that retained the design language of Gibson's carved archtops. The top was maple, a proven material for a guitar top, but it was glued to a mahogany body and a mahogany neck, and it had two of Gibson's proven P-90 pickups, both with volume and tone controls, and a pickup selector switch.

Paul loved the new guitar, and he loved that it would carry his name in a lucrative endorsement unusual for its time. The Gibson Les Paul, launched in 1952, and the many iterations that followed, was a huge success and propelled Gibson into a new direction of music. Where the archtops were primarily seen as jazz guitars, this new solid-body design was picked up by the rock-and-roll and blues players.

Among these was a young Delta blues player named John Lee Hooker, who was the son of a sharecropper. Hooker's career was just taking off when the Gibson Les Paul was introduced in 1952. It was

Guitars

John Lee Hooker on a rare British tour in 1955.

the perfect instrument for Hooker's brilliant, rhythm-forward blues guitar style.

Among other musicians closely associated with the Les Paul are Duane Allman and Eric Clapton, whose collaboration on the Derek and the Dominoes album *Layla and Other Assorted Love Songs* is considered a high point in both guitarists' careers. Some commentators believe that Clapton's playing on the Gibson Les Paul had a quality that he never achieved with his Fender Stratocasters. Jimmy Page played a Les Paul Gold Top, as did another great British guitarist, Peter Green. The list goes on—proof that the Gibson Les Paul, in continuous production since its launch in 1952, is one of the greatest guitars ever made.

Gibson Les Paul Old Black 1953

Type and body: Single-cutaway, solid-body electric guitar. Mahogany body. Maple top. Bigsby vibrato tailpiece.
Neck and Fingerboard: Mahogany neck. Rosewood fingerboard.
Pickups: Firebird bridge pickup and original P-90 neck pickup.

Sometimes a guitar transcends its own reputation to find a higher place in the myths, legends, and imaginations that are at the heart of popular culture. Such a guitar is Neil Young's 1953 Gibson Les Paul, nicknamed Old Black for the paint color that, at some time in its life, replaced the pristine Gold Top of its origin.

Gibson launched the Les Paul Gold Top in 1952, the year before Neil Young's guitar was built, and it had already undergone some modification by then, with a "stud" bar tailpiece that was anchored directly to the top instead of the Paul-designed tailpiece of 1952.

Neil Young's guitar is as beaten up as can be and is itself heavily modified. The original pickguard is long gone, replaced by a piece of light metal. The neck pickup is a corroded, but original, P-90, and somewhere along the way, it acquired a Gibson Tune-o-matic bridge. It sports a Bigsby, which is a cool nod to the times in which both the guitar and the Bigsby were built. Most of all, it has an unmistakably shabby vibe. And it is this ineffable sense of grunginess that became an inspiration to the young musicians in Seattle who would become the progenitors of the grunge movement, arguably the most important new movement of rock music in the late 1980s and 1990s.

This Gibson Les Paul is, to the eye, what the grunge guitar sound was to the ear. Muddy, fuzzy, distorted, and noisy. Where the heavy metal heroes indulged in hairdo guitar solos, the grunge players thrashed and bashed their way through their chords. Young acquired the guitar from his friend Buffalo Springfield bass player Jim Messina in 1968 and has used it more or less constantly ever since.

If rock music has guitar heroes, this 1953 Gibson Les Paul is its musical inversion: a hero guitar.

Neil Young in 1978.

Gretsch 6128 Duo Jet 1953

Type and body: Single-cutaway, solid-body with chambers electric guitar. Maple top. Mahogany body.
Neck and Fingerboard: Mahogany neck. Ebony fingerboard.
Pickups: Two DeArmond single-coil pickups.

The early 1950s was a frenzied period of electric guitar design and innovation. Paul Bigsby, making bespoke guitars and his vibrato tailpiece in Los Angeles; Fender with the Telecaster and Stratocaster models in nearby Fullerton, California; and Gibson, with its glorious Les Paul, made in Kalamazoo, Michigan. These makers hardly knew it, but they were changing the world.

In Brooklyn, the Gretsch company was in tune with the frenzy. When Leo Fender launched his Broadcaster, Fred Gretsch was quick to respond with a cease-and-desist letter, because Gretsch was using that trademark on some of its drums. Fender capitulated, of course, but Gretsch's approach was not just legal. Gretsch was responding to the new wave of guitars with a group of outstanding instruments of its own, all of which would make their mark on music in the United States and the rest of the world.

The Gretsch 6128, also known as the Duo Jet, was a direct response to Gibson's Les Paul. Gretsch realized that they needed to get a solid-body guitar to the market to respond to Fender, but more important was countering Gibson, whose Les Paul had the level of quality (and Les Paul's endorsement) that was instantly understood by Jimmie Webster, Gretsch's design and marketing genius. Webster, a great guitarist who had played with the Count Basie Orchestra, among other notables, understood professional guitar players and their needs.

The 6128 was called a Duo Jet by Webster, not only because of its two DeArmond pickups but also because Webster thought the association with the new jet age was cool. However, although Webster and Fred Gretsch saw it as their answer to the Les Paul, it was not actually a solid-body. It was a semi-hollow-body guitar, with voids and chambers that could be used to route cables and house electronics, and design innovations, including a bridge called the Melita Synchro-Sonic, that allowed each string to be fine-tuned at the bridge end, a great idea that was copied by Gibson with its Tune-o-matic bridge.

Paul McCartney has described his school friend George Harrison as a guitar freak. In fact, guitars were their common bond; they were both guitar aficionados. It was virtually impossible for British musicians to get their hands on decent American guitars, however, George managed to get his "first good guitar," a 1957 Duo Jet, when he responded to a newspaper ad placed by a young Liverpool merchant sailor returning from the United States. It was a good buy, and George used it on the Beatles' earliest recordings, including "Please Please Me," "I Want to Hold Your Hand," "I Saw Her Standing There," and "Twist and Shout." George Harrison later played several other guitars with the Beatles, including the Rickenbacker 360/12 twelve-string, both Stratocaster and Telecaster Fenders, and famously his Gretsch Country Gentleman.

The guitar pictured is a 1955 model.

Supro/Valco Dual-Tone 1954

Type and body: Single-cutaway, solid-body electric guitar. Plastic-covered basswood body.
Neck and Fingerboard: Aluminum tube core, wood, and plastic neck. Rosewood fingerboard.
Pickups: Two single-coil pickups.

There were several smaller excellent guitar makers in the United States during the second half of the twentieth century, and the best among them included Kay, Harmony, and Danelectro. The Valco company, based in Chicago and created by former owners of National Dobro, including Louis Dopyera, one of the original Dopyera brothers, made top-of-the-line amplifiers and guitars under the names Airline, National, and Supro.

Of these, Supro was by far the coolest-looking of all, with midcentury-modern lines that still look fabulous and contemporary. The guitars were not without their innovations, and they produced a great sound. Certainly, they were good enough for musicians of the caliber of Jimmy Page in England and Link Wray in California. The first unusual design element was the neck, which was bulky because it was built around an aluminum tube, with a rosewood fingerboard attached. The body, with its elegant, stepped tailpiece and its fabulous black-and-white pickguard, was made of wood covered in a form of plastic wrap. Later models had bodies made of fiberglass. With two single-coil

pickups done up to look like PAF humbuckers, the guitar sounded good, and the price was right.

Browsing on eBay one evening prior to a tour, David Bowie bought several Supro Dual-Tones and gave them to New York–based Dutch luthier Flip Scipio to "fluff up." They needed more than fluffing up; they needed to be completely rebuilt, which became a race against time for Scipio, who, by special request, also fitted a Bigsby to one. Bowie was well pleased and played them both on his concert tours and on recordings.

The guitar pictured is a model from about 1967.

Gibson ES-350T 1955

Type and body: Hollow-body electric guitar. Maple top, back, and sides.
Neck and Fingerboard: Maple neck. Rosewood fingerboard.
Pickups: Two Gibson P-90 pickups.

The 1950s saw a surge of optimism after the devastation of World War II. Cinema, theater, art, and music all saw enormous advances. The timing was perfect for Gibson, especially with their range of Electric Spanish archtop models, which started in the 1930s, went on hold during the privations of the 1940s, and came roaring back with rock and roll in the 1950s.

In 1948 the first of the modern electric archtop designs arrived, the ES-350, with its large, lush-sounding 17-inch (43-cm) body, a beautifully rounded Venetian single cutaway, and a pair of P-90 pickups. This design was a success, but with the dawn of rock and roll, the ES-350 needed an upgrade, and it got it in 1955 with the introduction of the ES-350T, the *T* standing for *Thinline*, meaning that the large body was made smaller, lighter, and somewhat easier to move around.

Timing is everything, and it was at this moment that Chuck Berry, one of the greatest guitarists of any era, burst onto the scene playing the ES-350T. Born in St. Louis, Berry grew up surrounded by music. Berry's older sister played classical piano and loved Beethoven. It says something of their sibling rivalry, not to mention Berry's sense of humor, that he had his sister in mind when he wrote one of his great hits, "Roll Over Beethoven."

Chuck Berry's talent was evident from an early age. He played and performed in high school, and after he got married, Berry began playing blues and "hillbilly" songs at night. Berry's interest in country music led to his first major hit, "Maybellene," which he recorded in 1955 using his Gibson ES-350T. Berry adapted the song from a country tune, "Ida Red," made popular by country star Bob Wills. Berry sold more than one million records with "Maybellene," and with its heady mix of country swing and piercing blues guitar lines, its success catapulted Berry into national and international fame. Widely credited as one of the fathers of rock and roll, Berry was also the first Black rock-and-roll artist to find widespread fame, and his success in the face of persistent racism is considered a breakthrough for Black artists since. With his brilliant guitar licks, his pulsing dance rhythms, and his raunchy, performing artistry, Berry's influence on popular music is profound. Artists including the Beatles and the Rolling Stones revered him. As Leonard Cohen famously said, "All of us are footnotes to the words of Chuck Berry."

The guitar pictured is a 1959 model that was owned by Chuck Berry.

Gretsch
White Falcon
1955

Type and body: Spruce-laminated hollow-body electric guitar. Maple back and sides.
Neck and Fingerboard: Maple neck. Ebony fingerboard.
Pickups: Two Gretsch DynaSonic pickups.

As the 1950s took hold, guitar music was on the rise. In 1951, the year Fender launched the Telecaster, guitarists Les Paul and Mary Ford had a hit with "How High the Moon," which featured bravura playing by Paul. Gibson launched its own solid-body guitar, the Les Paul, in 1952.

Gretsch, an old company with its headquarters in Brooklyn, took note of all this activity. When Gretsch issued a cease-and-desist order against Fender for using the name Broadcaster on its new guitar, what it really wanted to do was to get in on the action. The company did this by designing the Duo Jet, a solid-body electric guitar aimed squarely at the Fender and Gibson markets.

Gretsch's design genius was Jimmie Webster, himself an excellent musician as well as a great salesman. Using the New York City music scene as his backdrop, Webster launched his models at extravagant trade shows in Manhattan's Sheraton Hotel. Building on the success of the Duo Jet, and knowing the New York music scene as well as he did, he pushed his colleagues to build a deluxe

guitar, a luxurious guitar, a Cadillac of a guitar. Gretsch did so with the White Falcon. At first, it was meant to be a one-off simply to showcase Gretsch's design capabilities; however, such was the reaction that Gretsch rushed it into production, and it was an immediate success.

Everything about the White Falcon is fabulous. First, it was a big guitar, with a 17-inch (43-cm) hollow body finished in a brilliant white. The headstock had a pair of wings in sparkling gold (this guitar was a bird, after all), and it featured a falcon with outstretched wings etched onto the sparkling gold pickguard. The Grover tuners were gold-plated, and the gold tailpiece featured a G for *Gretsch* and a cast chevron evoking a pair of wings at speed.

Musicians have always flocked to the Falcon. During the heyday of Crosby, Stills, Nash & Young, both Neil Young and Stephen Stills played matching White Falcons. More recently, Bono has played a custom Irish Falcon—of course, painted green. But at its launch in 1954, one of Webster's coups was to have the wonderful, and since-overlooked, jazz guitarist Mary Osborne debut the guitar. You can hear Osborne's beautiful playing of this majestic musical bird wherever you stream your music.

Gretsch 6120 1955

Type and body: Single-cutaway, hollow-body electric guitar. Maple body.
Neck and Fingerboard: Mahogany neck. Rosewood fingerboard.
Pickups: Two single-coil DeArmond pickups.

Gibson's success with the Les Paul had a profound effect on other guitar makers, not least because the idea that a celebrity endorsement could have an effect on the sales of guitars was relatively new.

Jimmie Webster, Gretsch's design and marketing genius, was quick to recognize a trend and take full advantage of it. Chet Atkins was one of a few guitarists making an impact on popular music in the mid-1950s, so he seemed a natural choice for Gretsch. Webster developed what would become Atkins' signature model, the Gretsch 6120, released in 1955. And what a glorious guitar it was—a big hollow-body guitar with a single cutaway and the same gold-speckled, floating pickguard that was seen on the White Falcon.

The discussions between Atkins and Webster on exactly how the 6120 would look were apparently detailed and slightly acrimonious. Webster wanted to take advantage of the Atkins Nashville sound by including hokey cowboy details on the guitar. One of Atkins's nicknames was, after all, the Country Gentleman. But Atkins got his way, and

apart from the *G* brand on the lower body, the guitar is relatively unadorned. Atkins did insist on having a Bigsby fitted, over Webster's apparent objections, and the guitar was hardly subtle, with a flamboyant red color palette.

Feedback on electric guitars was a perennial problem, and part of Gretsch's solution was to paint black f-holes where the real things might have been. Subsequent versions of the guitar included the Country Gentleman and the Tennessean (the latter famously played by George Harrison), which featured Gretsch's own version of Gibson's humbucker pickups, called Filter'Trons.

The Atkins guitar sold well from the start, so much so that several years later, Atkins himself said creating the Atkins guitar was the best decision Jimmie Webster ever made.

Kay
Thin Twin K161
c.1955

Type and body: Semi-hollow-body electric guitar. Maple top and back. Mahogany sides.
Neck and Fingerboard: Maple neck. Rosewood fingerboard.
Pickups: Two Kay single-coil blade pickups (Thin Twin).

By the mid-1950s the major forces of guitar production and design were aligned, established, and flourishing. Gibson, with its range of acoustic, hollow-body, archtop, and solid-body guitars, was the behemoth. Fender's Telecaster and Stratocaster guitars were becoming both the sound and the image of rock and roll. With sales booming, other guitar makers were keen to join the party. Kay Musical Instrument Co. was formed in Chicago in 1931, out of the remnants of Stromberg-Voisinet, and by the 1950s it was producing a large range of instruments, both under its own name and for other brands. These included Silvertone, Airline, and Truetone, which was sold by Western Auto, a huge chain of auto parts stores. These guitars were not of high quality. Instead, they were deliberately made at a budget price to appeal to students, amateur musicians, and people who couldn't afford a Gibson or a Fender.

Perhaps because making these instruments at a budget price had an obvious consequence for their performance, the designers understood that for the guitars to sell, they really had to look good.

Today, Kay guitars from this era are sought after for their great midcentury design and performance that can, with some work and care, approach that of a good—even a very good—guitar.

Jimmy Reed was a blues guitarist whose influence on other artists was even bigger than the modest success he achieved in his own lifetime. The Rolling Stones recorded Reed's songs, as did Elvis Presley, and Van Morrison's original Belfast band Them. Reed is closely associated with this guitar, the Kay Thin Twin K161.

The Thin Twin looked fantastic, with its single cutaway, its signature pickguard, and two thin, and thin-sounding, pickups of Kay's own design. Kay had considerable success with this guitar, and with subsequent designs of higher quality, until the company finally folded in the mid-1960s.

Influential guitarist and producer Aaron Dessner appeared on the 2021 Grammy Awards with Jack Antonoff, accompanying Taylor Swift. Dessner was playing a Kay flattop, a moment that thrust Kay into a renewed spotlight and elevated it to a level of cool hitherto unlikely for such a modest guitar.

Premier
E-722 Ruby Special
c.1955

Type and body: Single-cutaway, solid-body
painted electric guitar. Mahogany body.
Neck and Fingerboard: Mahogany neck. Brazilian
rosewood fingerboard.
Pickups: Two Franz single-coil pickups.

As the 1950s exploded with new singers, new
bands, and new guitarists, the mainstream guitar
makers could hardly keep pace with the demand
for guitars. Into the market came several guitar
companies that sought to supply good-quality
budget guitars to meet the voracious demand.
Some of these makers—particularly United, Kay,
Danelectro, and Harmony—supplied guitars
under different brand names, often the brands of
the large mail-order companies that were a deep
part of the American retail culture in the postwar
period. These companies would brand the guitars
as their own, and never attained the renown of
the leading brands, such as Fender and Gibson.
After being forgotten for so long, the best of these
guitars are now being reevaluated. Among the
very best is this Premier, manufactured by United
Guitars in Hoboken, New Jersey, for the Sorkin
Music Company of New York City.

Sorkin's Premier guitars are now both rare and
in demand. The arrangement with United was
unusual. United was a manufacturing wholesaler.
Sorkin purchased the bodies, and possibly necks,
and added the various accoutrements required to
make a complete guitar. The result was a testament to the great Italian craftsmen at United,
whose skills as luthiers grew out of their artisanal
connection to some of the best Italian mandolins
of the nineteenth century.

This guitar, owned by guitarist and producer John
Leventhal, is a solid-body of beautiful painted
mahogany, with a Brazilian rosewood fingerboard
and unusual Franz single-coil pickups. Now in
great demand, Franz pickups were less expensive
versions of Gibson's P-90 pickups and were used
on early Guilds, as well as on Premier guitars.

Among the musicians who played Premier was
Mark Sandman, the bassist and founder of influential indie rock band Morphine, from Cambridge,
Massachusetts. Sandman played his Premier bass
with a slide, and either one or two strings. The body
of his bass was exactly the same as this guitar, with
its characteristic Italianate scroll on the upper body,
a look back to the mandolins of Orville Gibson.

Höfner
500/1 Bass
1956

Type and body: Semi-hollow-body electric bass guitar. Spruce top. Maple back and sides.
Neck and Fingerboard: Maple neck. Rosewood fingerboard.
Pickups: Two Höfner 511B violin bass pickups.

The 1950s was a grim period in British history. The country was deep in debt after World War II, especially to the United States. And import taxes, called tariffs, were in place that would make importing American goods all but impossible. For British musicians, this meant buying a range of European and Japanese instruments sometimes of lower quality.

One firm, Karl Höfner, sold excellent stringed instruments: violins, double basses, guitars, and ukuleles. Höfner is an old company, founded in 1887, and it was one of the biggest and best manufacturers of stringed instruments in Europe, and a favorite of British musicians.

Höfner introduced the 500/1 bass at the Frankfurt Music Fair in 1956, and it was, as you might expect, a cross between a cello and an acoustic guitar, with electronics embedded within. It was shaped like a cello but had no f-holes, making it essentially a semi-hollow-body guitar. It was well made and used good tone woods: spruce top, ma-ple body, and rosewood fingerboard. And because of its hollow body, it was light, although not very well balanced. Best of all, for such a good instrument, it was relatively inexpensive.

None of this would have made it famous were it not for a remarkable coincidence. By 1960, the Beatles were playing regular gigs in Hamburg, on the northern coast of Germany. Stuart Sutcliffe had left the band to pursue his art studies, and since both John Lennon and George Harrison refused to take Sutcliffe's place on bass, it was left to Paul McCartney to fill in. The trouble was, McCartney didn't own a bass guitar. He went to a music store and picked up the 500/1. As a left-hander, McCartney hated the look of an electric guitar "the wrong way around," with its cutaway upside down when played left-handed. The Höfner, however, with no cutaway, looked perfectly symmetrical. It sounded great, too, with a deep bass thrum from its two Höfner humbucker pickups that contributed to the Beatles' unique guitar sound. That first McCartney Höfner was a 1961 model, followed by a 1963 model two years later.

The Höfner 500/1 became the most famous bass guitar in the world, played by the most famous, and most brilliant, player of his time. It is still in production more than sixty years later.

Paul McCartney with his famous violin bass, and Ringo keeping time, in 1964.

Antoria/Guyatone LG-50 c.1957

Type and body: Single-cutaway, solid-body electric guitar. Maple body.
Neck and Fingerboard: Maple neck. Rosewood fingerboard.
Pickups: Two Guyatone single-coil pickups.

The 1950s was a difficult decade for musicians in Great Britain. The post-World War II economy was lumbering slowly back to life, aided by import tariffs on U.S. goods, which made American guitars virtually impossible to buy. Meanwhile, the Japanese guitar company Guyatone was making reasonably good, budget instruments under the direction of founder and designer Mitsuo Matsuki. Just as the large American companies did, Matsuki allowed his instruments to be rebranded by the dealers and importers in other countries. J. T. Coppock was an import company based in Leeds, in northeast England, and it used the brand name Antoria on various imported goods, including Guyatone guitars.

Guyatone guitars were built completely by Matsuki and his team, including the electronics, which featured Matsuki's own pickups. The LG-50 was a midrange electric guitar with two pickups, and it caught the eye of eighteen-year-old British virtuoso Hank Marvin. At about the time that Marvin acquired this guitar, he moved to London with his best friend to try to break into the music scene. In a Soho coffee shop, Marvin met the manager of an equally young singer, Cliff Richard, who asked Marvin if he would like to front Richard's new band. Thus was born the Shadows (the band's first name, the Drifters, was quickly dropped), which enjoyed huge success both on its own account and as the backing band for Richard. As Richard's star rose, so did Marvin's, and he had a British No. 1 hit record in 1960 with his guitar instrumental "Apache." Whether backing Richard or on their own, Marvin and the Shadows were a ubiquitous presence in British pop music of the 1960s and the early 1970s.

The story is well-known that, with his first success, Richard—famously generous—bought Marvin a brand-new red Fender Stratocaster, a guitar that became closely identified with Marvin's sound and the sound of the Shadows. But it was with this modest guitar, the Antoria LG-50, that Marvin, along with a generation of British guitarists of the 1950s and early 1960s, first made his mark.

Aldens/Harmony H-45 Stratotone 1958

Type and body: Single-cutaway, hollow-body electric guitar. Laminated maple body.
Neck and Fingerboard: Maple neck. Ebonized maple fingerboard.
Pickups: One single-coil pickup.

Guitar fans, both musicians and collectors, have for some time been alert to the possibility that many of the obscure brands of electric guitars are worth playing and owning. The Harmony Guitar Company was hardly obscure. At its height, the Chicago factory was producing thousands of instruments a week, many for its owner, Sears, Roebuck & Co., the largest mail-order company in the United States at the time, under its own brand, Silvertone. At its demise in 1975, Harmony had produced more than ten million guitars and many other ukuleles, banjos, and violins.

What sets Harmony guitars apart is the sense of design that imbues the instruments. Whether archtops, solid-bodies, or acoustics, design details abound. The shape of a bridge or a tailpiece, for example, as on the archtops. In honor of Charles Lindberg, one bridge was designed as an aircraft.

The H-45 Stratotone was Harmony's best electric guitar. Its fluid, modernist design qualities seem timeless six decades after it was first produced with a single cutaway; a large, amorphous pick-guard; and either one or two pickups, produced by Rowe Industries in Ohio. Harmony also produced the Stratotone for Aldens, the large catalog company. Curiously, Aldens didn't rebrand their guitars, other than printing an ornate *H* on the headstock. These Aldens Stratotones are now considered to be among the most collectible of all.

Today, the Harmony Stratotone is considered to have a perfect garage band sound: tinny, twangy, piercing. Most Stratotones are now refurbished with improved electronics, most often the pickups, which were one of the guitar's weak spots.

British guitarist, singer, songwriter, and producer Lianne La Havas found fame for her recordings, live performances, and subtle electric guitar playing style. La Havas is also known for her collection of guitars, including a lovely single-pickup Aldens's H-45 Stratotone. In an earlier generation, singer-guitarist Ritchie Valens played virtually the same guitar, an H-44 Stratotone, which can be heard on most of his recordings.

Lianne La Havas playing one of several Stratotones she owns in 2016.

Danelectro Longhorn 1958

Type and body: Double-cutaway, hollow-body electric guitar. Poplar body. Masonite top and back. Taped sides.
Neck and Fingerboard: Stapled poplar neck. Pau ferro fingerboard.
Pickups: Two Danelectro single-coil pickups in lipstick tubes.

Danelectro was founded in New Jersey in 1947 to produce budget amplifiers for large department stores under the Silvertone and Airline names. Nat Daniel, the founder, quickly followed with budget guitars, first for Sears, Roebuck & Co., the giant mail-order company, and then under the Danelectro name.

Daniel's guitar design was the work of a genius. Constrained by the need to create a good-looking, playable electric guitar for the lowest possible cost, he came up with the idea of making the body shape out of poplar, the cheapest industrial wood, traditionally used for making matchsticks, then bonding colored Masonite hardboard to the front and back. Daniel didn't bother finishing the side of the body other than to cover it with hardware store electrical tape.

What distinguished the guitars were the luscious body shapes, forms undreamed of by Gibson, Fender, or any of the other major guitar makers. The twin pickups of Daniel's own design were housed in tubes acquired from lipstick makers.

And the tan-and-cream sunburst color scheme was unlike anything else at the time. To top it all, Daniel's guitars were notable for the shape of the headstock, copied from the design of a Coke bottle.

Daniel's other great innovation was in the guitar's neck and fingerboard. In the Guitarlin, for example, the neck has thirty-one frets, allowing for the player to explore the upper register of the instrument in ways impossible on any other guitar. With the Silvertone brand contracted to Sears, Roebuck & Co. selling in large numbers, and his own brand Danelectro selling well, business boomed well into the 1960s, and the range of instruments grew. The Guitarlin was uniquely a six-stringed bass, with the upper register sounding like an electric guitar. The Longhorn came as either a bass or a six-string. The Silvertone, made for Sears, with a black body and a large white pickguard, was popular for its striking looks alone, and is now highly collectible.

The list of guitarists who play Danelectro guitars is like a who's who of the greatest players in the last half century. Guitar innovator Link Wray favored Danelectro guitars, probably because they were affordable and played well. Hugely influential, Wray pioneered the use of the power chord, one of the essential building blocks of guitar rock music. His hit song "Rumble" was both banned, lest it incite gang violence, and revered by guitarists as diverse as Jimmy Page, Pete Townshend, and Neil Young, not to mention a generation of punk rockers. Perhaps it is because he identified as Native American or Indigenous that Wray has largely been ignored by the mainstream. Perhaps it is because of his deliberately "outsider" persona. Whatever the reasons, it is high time that Link Wray is recognized as the influential guitarist that he unquestionably was.

Gibson ES-355 1958

Type and body: Double-cutaway, semi-hollow-body electric guitar. Maple body.
Neck and Fingerboard: Mahogany neck. Ebony fingerboard.
Pickups: Two Gibson humbucker pickups.

Gibson's hollow-body electric guitars were renowned for their beautiful tone—luscious, warm, and moody. But their very hollowness made them notoriously prone to feedback when the volume knob was turned up high.

From 1952, Gibson had been producing the Les Paul, a solid-body guitar with incredible tone that was virtually impervious to feedback. The answer to the hollow-body feedback problem seemed clear. In a throwback to Les Paul's Log, where Paul ran a four-by-four down the length of the body and attached two "wings" to the top and bottom to make up the shape of the guitar, the ES-335 has a solid piece of maple that runs through the center of the body, with the two hollow portions forming the top and bottom of the guitar body, making it a semi-hollow-body. Thus the feedback problem was solved and the guitar retained the rich tone and sustain of the earlier ES models. Produced in 1958, with two f-holes, a double cutaway, and two humbucker pickups, the ES-335 was an instant success and appealed to jazz players, rockers, and blues players alike. Upgrades to the woods, the

hardware, and the detailing quickly brought the ES-345 and the ES-355.

B. B. King took up the ES-355 and played a succession of them, all called Lucille. Born in rural Mississippi, King was raised by his grandmother and was interested in music from the start. A common theme for the early rock and blues performers, from Chuck Berry and Jerry Lee Lewis to Little Richard and Fats Domino, was the role of church music in their musical education. King was no different. He sang in the church choir, where, according to legend, the minister played a Silvertone guitar. His biography will say that he was one generation removed from the "field hollers" of the Deep South. Field hollers weren't folksy country tunes; instead, they were the existential cries of the deep pain of slavery. Those cries are heard in every note sung by King, who was born a scant generation after slavery's end.

According to one story, King was given his first guitar by one of the church ministers, but it wasn't until later in life, when he followed his cousin to Memphis and first saw T-Bone Walker, that King decided to devote himself to the electric guitar.

King's fluid solos—played with beautiful, bent-string vibratos, clearly picked phrasing, and a silky tone—came to define the modern electric guitar blues style. Along with his sonorous church-choir baritone, King enjoyed a long career, touring and recording constantly. He claimed to have been the first Black artist invited to play in Las Vegas, introduced by his friend Frank Sinatra. Look for his concert at Sing Sing prison in Ossining, New York, recorded in 1972, which shows King's humor, his great singing, and his brilliant blues guitar style.

The guitar pictured is a 1959 model.

Gibson Explorer 1958

Type and body: Single-cutaway, solid-body electric guitar. Korina body.
Neck and Fingerboard: Korina neck. Rosewood fingerboard.
Pickups: Two Gibson PAF humbucker pickups.

Ted McCarty is one of the production design geniuses of Gibson's post–World War II era. McCarty was responsible for persuading Les Paul to add his name to Gibson's new 1952 solid-body guitar, designed by John Huis, a guitar that came to define the highest standard of electric guitar design. By the mid-1950s, with the Les Paul selling well, the archtops increasingly seen as jazz guitars, and the Gibson SG still several years away, McCarty decided to add "modern" designs to Gibson's range. There were to be three new models: the Flying V, the Moderne, and the Explorer.

The Flying V was a gorgeous guitar that sang the chords of the new space age, and although a failure to begin with, it found fame when reintroduced in the following decades. The Moderne never went into production, at least not until a couple of decades later. The Explorer was a flop, selling fewer than fifty guitars before production was halted. McCarty had designed these guitars himself, and their failure was a blow, both to Gibson and to McCarty personally. That the guitar failed has nothing to do with its quality, with a gorgeous, angular body; two PAF humbucker pickups; and a headstock in the shape of a drooping hockey stick, variations of which would reappear both at Gibson and at other guitar makers over the years.

Gradually, the conservative tastes of guitar players of the time gave way to the kind of design bravura that McCarty brought to his Futura line of guitars, which is how they are now described. The Explorer was brought back into production in 1976, where it has remained, on and off, to this day.

The story is well known: In the late 1970s, a teenage Dave Evans, on vacation with his family from his home in Dublin, went into a guitar store in New York City with the intention of spending his savings on a Les Paul. Instead, this funny-looking modern guitar caught his eye, and he asked to try it out. He was smitten and purchased the guitar, a 1976 Gibson Explorer. When he got back to Dublin, he showed his pals Larry Mullen Jr., Adam Clayton, and Paul Hewson his new guitar, and they loved it for both its look and its sound. Hewson became Bono, Evans became the Edge, and the band became U2.

It is no exaggeration to say that the Edge is one of the greatest guitar players of all time and—along with Jimmy Page, Jimi Hendrix, Chuck Berry, Jack White, Johnny Marr, and a handful of others—one of the great innovators of rock music. The Edge eschews the flashy, macho solos of Page and his followers, instead creating sonic landscapes that define the very essence of a U2 song. His use of spare chord voicings, dotted echoes, and intricate harmonic shapes have changed the sound of rock guitar music from the 1980s on.

The Edge plays his 1976 Gibson Explorer on many of U2's earliest recordings and on their hit single "Beautiful Day," from U2's 2000 album *All That You Can't Leave Behind.* Listen to the Edge's unmistakable sound and savor the playing of a musical savant.

Edge playing his first great guitar, purchased in a New York guitar store, in 1985.

Gibson Flying V 1958

Type and body: Solid-body electric guitar.
Korina body.
Neck and Fingerboard: Korina neck.
Rosewood fingerboard.
Pickups: Two Gibson PAF humbucker pickups.

Of all the guitars that Gibson has designed, the Flying V was the most radical. It was, however, too radical for the times, and after a short run beginning in 1958, the model was discontinued, only to be reintroduced much later, when tastes were loosening and guitarists were becoming more adventurous. Gibson president Ted McCarty could not be blamed for trying modernist designs. This was the space age, after all, and futuristic rocket shapes were appearing successfully in everything from clocks to chairs to restaurant architecture. Of the three futuristic designs McCarty initiated, only two made it into production: the Flying V and the Explorer, both now highly prized.

The development of both the shape and materials of the Flying V took Gibson in several new directions at once. After trying mahogany for the body, only to find it way too heavy, they settled on African korina wood, which was hard and light, perfect properties for a guitar body.

Two of the early enthusiasts for the Flying V were Albert King and country rock pioneer Lonnie Mack, the latter owning the seventh Flying V off the production line. King's career, which began in Arkansas before he ended up in Memphis, is a story of struggle and success, often mixed together. What was always there was his blues playing, which had the plaintive sob of his tough childhood in every lick, in every wide vibrato note.

Dave Davies of the Kinks was another early Flying V player, but it wasn't until the glam metal craze emerged in Great Britain and the United States in the 1970s that the guitar had a second life, which has continued in an on-again, off-again fashion ever since.

Fender Telecaster 1959

Type and body: Single-cutaway, solid-body electric guitar. Ash body.
Neck and Fingerboard: Maple neck. Rosewood fingerboard.
Pickups: Two Fender single-coil pickups.

By the beginning of the 1960s, Fender was clearly the guitar of choice for rock guitarists. Players were split more or less equally between devotion to the Stratocaster or its sisters the Esquire and the Telecaster, but Fender owned the market. Gibson had its Les Paul, of course, and a line of beautiful Electric Spanish archtops, but it was really Fender all the way for guitarists in all genres from country to western swing to the emerging revolution of rock and roll. These players turned away from the jazz tones of the Gibsons toward the twangy, country tones of Fender's solid-body guitar. It was not fancy; just a plain vanilla guitar with no frills but tons of stripped-down attitude.

As the Telecaster built a following during the 1950s, some of the greatest guitarists of the era chose it, including Jimmy Bryant and James Burton. It was Burton's endorsement, and his virtuoso country-style playing of the guitar, that solidified its reputation among professional guitarists.

The Telecaster started as the Broadcaster, a name coined by Leo Fender's partner, Don Randall. After a false start (see page 114), the Broadcaster name gave way to the Telecaster, which was an even better name, evoking the new television era. By 1959, the Telecaster had, year by year, undergone several important upgrades, including better pickups.

Another guitarist drawn to the sound of the Tele was Jimmy Page, who was in the studio recording Led Zeppelin's fourth album when he began composing the various parts of an anthemic set of variations for guitar, "Stairway to Heaven." With several sections, and lasting a shade longer than eight minutes, "Stairway to Heaven" is not really a single song; instead, it is a series of nuanced sonic experiments on acoustic twelve-string and electric guitar that build and pulse, accelerate and swell into what Page himself describes as a "fanfare" hammered on the D chord, which introduces his climactic one-minute solo. Robert Plant's magical mystery lyrics, and his powerfully beautiful vocal performance add a linear coherence to the piece, and John Bonham's drum fills bring an explosive drive. However, it is Page's guitar playing that energizes "Stairway to Heaven" from the first bar to the last (allowing for Plant's hymnlike coda).

When it came to recording the guitar solo, Jimmy Page used his 1959 Telecaster, a gift from his close friend and fellow Londoner Jeff Beck. Although Page used this Tele for several years, he may be better known for his first guitar, a Futurama Grazioso, one of those inexpensive guitars popular in England in the 1950s, and his custom Gibson Les Paul.

Over the decades since the release of "Stairway to Heaven," the song has gone from greatest rock song ever to jaded dinosaur to *Wayne's World* ridicule to staple of AOR radio. Today, it is being reassessed. Page himself is restored as one of the great musical guitarist-innovators of late twentieth-century rock music. And "Stairway to Heaven" is now seen as something approaching a contemporary-music art-performance piece.

Robert Plant sings while Jimmy Page plays his Telecaster in 1969.

Gibson ES-175 1960

Type and body: Single-cutaway, hollow-body electric jazz guitar. Maple-laminated top. Maple back and sides.
Neck and Fingerboard: Mahogany neck. Rosewood fingerboard.
Pickups: One or two P-90 pickups.

The Gibson ES-175 was introduced in 1949 as a relatively budget version of Gibson's deluxe archtop models, and it quickly found its mark. Made with a laminate top instead of the carved top of its more expensive brethren, it was easy to produce, allowing it to be sold at an attractive price. It was named for that price, $175, and was not only lovely looking, with its elegant, sharp Florentine cutaway, but it sounded great, too, coming with a single pickup and a Tune-o-matic bridge. A second pickup quickly followed, and soon the guitar could be bought with two humbucker pickups as standard, making it a versatile instrument for all types of music. It was such a success that it continued in production for almost seventy years before being dropped in 2019 in favor of more contemporary designs.

It was the jazz guys who really took to the ES-175 throughout the 1950s and 1960s. Herb Ellis was one of the first, acquiring a 1953 instrument that he played during his time with Oscar Peterson while also backing Ella Fitzgerald and many others. The list of ES-175 players goes on, including B. B. King for a while, Keith Richards, and Mark Knopfler.

Pat Metheny acquired an ES-175 as a teenager and used it throughout his early career as a teacher, a player, and a recording artist. Some of his earliest recordings for ECM include landmark albums *Bright Size Life* (1976), *Watercolors* (1977), and *Pat Metheny Group* (1978). Joni Mitchell toured in support of her album *Mingus* in 1979, and she said at the time that she wanted the tour to be "considered a musical event." Along with Jaco Pastorius on his Fender fretless bass, Lyle Mays on keyboards, and Don Alias on percussion, Joni Mitchell chose Metheny to play the guitar. She chose well in Metheny, whose playing on his ES-175 is wonderful. Whether he is playing fast, harmonic scales, extraordinarily complex chords with unique voicings, or simpler single-note meditations on his high E string, every note glows with emotion as pervasive and beautiful as the morning dew on a flower.

The Mitchell tour was a big success and led to the 1980 live album *Shadows and Light*. Pat Metheny's playing is incandescent on every track, but his singular "Pat's Solo" shows him at his improvisatory best, playing his beloved ES-175. The guitar, by this stage, had been heavily used and sported a toothbrush holding Metheny's strap and a piece of duct tape covering the hole where the bridge pickup had been (it had fallen out previously). No matter, Metheny's brilliant, emotional, plaintive, contemporary jazz guitar style is on full display throughout, and is a perfect foil to Mitchell's own brilliance, both on vocals and playing her own Ibanez George Benson guitar.

Pat Metheny bought his guitar used in 1968 for $100.

Kay
Value Leader
1960

Type and body: Single-cutaway, semi-hollow-body thinline electric guitar. Wood fiberboard body.
Neck and Fingerboard: Maple neck. Rosewood fingerboard.
Pickups: Three Kay single-coil "pancake" pickups.

The Kay Musical Instrument Company grew, in part, out of what had been Stromberg-Voisinet, maker of some of the best guitars created in the early part of the twentieth century. It should be no surprise that Kay would itself become a noted producer of excellent guitars.

The Thin Twin K161 was one of Kay's most successful electric guitars, played by Jimmy Reed, among many other great guitarists. The top-of-the-line Barney Kessel Pro is also unquestionably a great guitar. However, the Value Leader, one of Kay's "budget" electric guitars was popular, not least because of its price. Available in various configurations of one, two, or three pickups, the Value Leader was favored by blues players, including the great Lonnie Johnson.

The Value Leader, like all Kay instruments, had the feeling that it was a designed object rather than something that just emerged from a factory. Admittedly inexpensive, it sported a simple long, metal pickguard, which also anchored its controls. With a single Florentine cutaway, the body looked sharp. With a maple neck and fingerboard and a classic headstock featuring a single *K* with an Art Deco surround, the guitar looked much better than its price might have suggested.

Lonnie Johnson was a leader both of jazz and blues guitar playing; however, he began with the blues in his native New Orleans. After moving to Chicago, Johnson had a successful career, performing, touring, and recording with some of the jazz greats of the day, including Louis Armstrong and Duke Ellington. On a tour in Great Britain in the early 1950s, a young skiffle player changed his name in honor of Johnson, finding his own fame as Lonnie Donegan. In spite of Johnson's relative success, and the enormous influence he had on musicians of all genres, including a young Bob Dylan, he barely eked out a living. After a long career, Johnson died in poverty at the age of seventy-one. It is too often written that blues players preferred less expensive guitars for their "earthy" tones. How about this: Blues players, mostly Black men and some women, could not afford fancy guitars. For many years, Wes Montgomery, the greatest jazz guitarist of his time, subsidized his music by working a day job as a welder. If that was the economic reality for a top-flight jazz musician of the mid-twentieth century, the lot of a blues player was even more precarious.

Kay guitars have become both fashionable and collectible, with the best competing with vintage instruments by Fender, Gibson, and others. Guitarist and producer Aaron Dessner appeared at the Grammys accompanying Taylor Swift on a vintage Kay acoustic guitar.

Fender Jazzmaster 1961

Type and body: Double-cutaway, solid-body electric guitar. Alder body. Fender vibrato tailpiece.
Neck and Fingerboard: Maple neck. Rosewood Fingerboard.
Pickups: Two single-coil pickups.

As sales of Fender's Telecaster and Stratocaster grew during the 1950s, Fender's head of sales, Don Randall, realized that the company was ignoring one important sector of the market: jazz. Leo Fender thought the answer would be an upmarket solid-body guitar, with softer tones to compete both with the Gibson archtops and, to a lesser extent, with the solid-body Les Paul.

Randall came up with the name and Freddie Tavares drew up the Jazzmaster, giving it an exaggerated, elongated shape. The look has been described as having an "offset waist," and the ostensible reason was that jazz players would find it more comfortable to play than either the Tele or the Strat. Ever the design modernist, Fender described the guitar's form as "a matter of fitting it to the ribcage, a matter of function."

Although not a trained designer or draftsman, Tavares had a genius for shape and form, and he imbued his Jazzmaster shape with echoes of a cartoon rocket ship, in perfect tune with the space-age 1950s and early 1960s. Tavares made his Jazzmaster look different and perfect, with a timeless design that still looks modern six decades later. In addition to the new shape, the Jazzmaster was given a rosewood fingerboard, a big change from the maple fingerboards that had almost become signatures of the Tele and Strat.

Fender wanted the guitar to sound much, much better than the Stratocaster, to be an altogether better—and pricier—guitar. Electronics expert that Fender was, he started with the electronics, which were a huge leap up from the earlier Fender electronics. He created two new pickups for the Jazzmaster, flat and wide, and new switches and controls, to give the guitarist much more control over the combinations of pickups, volume, and tone. The result was a beautifully mellow jazz tone in the neck pickup but a brighter, rockier tone when the pickups were selected together.

The guitar flopped with jazz players, content to stay with their gorgeous, beautiful-sounding arch-tops, ignoring Fender's mellow tones. It did find an audience, however, and the guitar has evolved over the years to become a solid citizen in the Fender range. Except for a hiatus in the 1980s, the Jazzmaster has been in production ever since.

Many notable guitarists have chosen the Jazzmaster ahead of other guitars, including Thurston Moore and Lee Ranaldo of Sonic Youth, who made the Jazzmaster almost a mascot of their band and reinvigorated the instrument for a generation of guitar players. Aaron Dessner of the National, a guitar aficionado as well as a great guitarist, plays his 1963 Jazzmaster brilliantly. Sean Eden, of New York indie band Luna, has played his 1964 Jazzmaster for thirty years and says it has "the ultimate electric guitar tone." Eden also says of the proprietary Fender vibrato system that "it is [his] favorite of any guitar, smooth and wavy, easily adjustable, stays in tune, and just feels easy to connect with musically."

Fender Stratocaster 1961

Type and body: Double-cutaway, solid-body electric guitar. Ash body.
Neck and Fingerboard: Maple neck. Rosewood fingerboard.
Pickups: Three Fender single-coil pickups.

By the early 1960s, the Fender Stratocaster was the default electric guitar for any young rock-and-roller. In the United States, pictures of Buddy Holly with his sunburst Stratocaster, and in Great Britain pictures of Hank Marvin and his red Strat—to mention just two greats—had fired the imaginations of countless young guitarists.

It is worth remembering, however, that by 1960 the Strat was not even ten years old. The design of the Stratocaster began in Fender's factory in south Los Angeles. Just after the initial success of the Telecaster, Leo Fender, always alert to the views of working musicians, believed he could improve the Tele. Don Randall, Fender's head of sales, saw a more urgent threat: Gibson's Les Paul. Randall saw the Telecaster as a "plain Jane instrument" that did not look good side by side with the luscious gold carved top of the Les Paul.

Fender got to work on his new design ideas. Joined by new employee and local guitarist Freddie Tavares, the team got to work on a new guitar. Tavares was a great addition to the team. Besides being a smart designer, he was a wonderful guitarist. For those interested in such things, Tavares's pop culture legend is secure because of the opening Hawaiian guitar "swoop" on the *Merrie Melodies* cartoon series.

Fender and Tavares had simple design imperatives: First, the guitar had to be more comfortable than the hard-edged Telecaster for a professional musician to hold and play. Next, and ever alert to what Paul Bigsby was doing in nearby downtown Los Angeles, Fender wanted his new guitar to have a vibrato device. Not the big, cast aluminum, visually dominant machine that was the Bigsby. Something smaller, with cool engineering, more accurate for tuning and tone, more refined. And Tavares wanted to add a pickup with qualities that would give more tonal options than the Telecaster. Fender was, first and foremost, an electronics guy, who knew what he was looking for and knew how to get there. The magic number of pickups was three, cleverly angled and at different heights to the strings, to give more tonal options than on any other electric guitar.

Fender and Tavares came up with the body shape, Tavares sketching it on a piece of paper that had lines for strings and another line for the bridge. His sketch led to one of the greatest, most popular, and most copied designs of all time—simple, elegant, perfect. Leo lifted another design cue from Bigsby: the enlarged area on the headstock where he could put the Fender name. Fender's tremolo was his pièce de résistance, an engineering marvel—small, accurate, beautifully engineered. The design of a sure-handed modernist, it has remained a Fender signature from that day to this.

By 1964, the Stratocaster was a runaway success, so much so that demand greatly outstripped supply. The city of Cork sits on the south coast of Ireland and was home to a teenage prodigy desperate for his first decent guitar. Rory Gallagher already had a guitar, a cheap one, given to him by

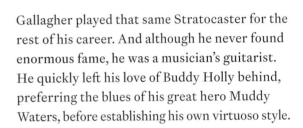

his parents. But looking at pictures of Buddy Holly, Gallagher wanted a Stratocaster. One appeared in the window of Crowley's Music Centre in the middle of Cork, and fifteen-year-old Gallagher had to have it. It was a 1961 model, reputedly the first Stratocaster ever imported into Ireland, and had belonged to the lead guitarist of the famous Royal Showband, who needed a guitar the same color as the band's outfits and not this sunburst model. The price tag was steep: one hundred pounds. Gallagher saved for the deposit and paid off the balance in installments, all the while working steadily as a prodigy guitar player for local showbands who played covers of popular hits.

Gallagher played that same Stratocaster for the rest of his career. And although he never found enormous fame, he was a musician's guitarist. He quickly left his love of Buddy Holly behind, preferring the blues of his great hero Muddy Waters, before establishing his own virtuoso style.

Gibson SG 1961

Type and body: Double-cutaway, solid-body electric guitar. Mahogany body. Early models with optional Gibson Vibrola tailpiece.
Neck and Fingerboard: Mahogany neck. Ebony fingerboard.
Pickups: Three Gibson PAF humbucker pickups.

It is hard to imagine from today's perspective, but the Gibson Les Paul was not always the runaway success we have come to understand as an eternal truth. By the end of the 1950s, Gibson's great rock-and-roll guitar was out of favor, soundly beaten in musicians' affections by Fender's trio of Stratocaster, Telecaster, and Esquire.

To add to the misery, Les Paul himself had fallen out of favor with the public, with his endorsement of Gibson's great guitar no longer being valuable. Something had to be done, and the result was the SG. Ironically—given that the Les Paul was a solid-body, albeit with a carved top—the SG stood for *Solid Guitar*, as if to reinforce the fact that it could go head-to-head with Strats and Teles. Even more odd is that the SG was seen by Gibson as a natural development of the Les Paul, not something new. History shows that the SG, with its thinner neck; thinner, flat body; double cutaway; and mahogany flat top—and a choice of two or three PAF humbucker pickups—was something entirely new. The SG was, and is, a beautiful guitar, and the original came in a rich pearl white with a white pickguard.

It is impossible to overstate the influence Sister Rosetta Tharpe has had on rock-and-roll music, and on rock guitar playing. Tharpe was born the daughter of cotton-picking parents in the aptly named town of Cotton Plant, Arkansas. Along with her mother, she was a church musician, and she began her career firmly in gospel music. The guitar was her instrument of choice, and gradually she added rhythm and blues to her repertoire.

Tharpe was equally comfortable playing in both clubs and churches. Her music has deep roots in the blues, as does gospel, and it is Tharpe's bluesy voice, along with her guitar prowess, that characterizes her music. Tharpe toured Great Britain in 1964 with a who's who of blues and R&B artists, including Sonny Terry, Brownie McGhee, and Muddy Waters. During this British tour, Tharpe gave a concert on a railroad station platform, recorded by the Manchester-based Granada Television. It is a stunningly powerful performance, luckily preserved, during which she plays her white 1961 Gibson SG Custom with a Vibrola tailpiece.

Sister Rosetta Tharpe playing her SG Custom in 1964.

Guitars

Wandré Rock Oval 1961

Type and body: Single-cutaway, solid-body electric guitar. Fiberglass body over wood.
Neck and Fingerboard: Aluminum neck. Rosewood fingerboard.
Pickups: Two single-coil pickups.

One downside to the dominance of American electric guitar builders, such as Gibson and Fender, is that it seems to have stifled guitar design innovation, not to mention competition, from elsewhere in the world. Italian luthier and production designer Antonio Pioli bucked this trend with a large range of marvelous, if eccentric, electric guitars, as well as double basses, bass guitars, and even mandolins, under the Wandré name. Pioli's father, Roberto Pioli, was a luthier in the fine Italian tradition, with a workshop in Cavriago, a small Italian town between Parma and Bologna. Pioli learned his lutherie in his father's workshop, where he earned his nickname, Wandré, which apparently means "walking backward" in Reggiano dialect. Pioli may have been moving against the crowd, but he learned his craft well, and his guitars are now highly prized and desirable, treasured for their shapes, colors, styles, and sound.

It is almost invidious to single out just one guitar from Pioli's eleven-year career making guitars with the Wandré name. This guitar, the Rock Oval, is one of Pioli's best-known designs. It has a lovely fluid, amoebic shape, two single-coil pickups, and other electronics of Pioli's own design, along with an aluminum neck with a rosewood fingerboard. The body is interesting, made of resin-covered wood. However, it is the colors that are especially appealing, showing Pioli's undoubted gifts as an artist and echoing fellow Italian designer Gaetano Pesce's experiments with colored resins. Pioli, voraciously well read, would have known about Pesce's work, just as he identified with the Fluxus art movement in full flow during his heyday. It is said that the Rock Oval is inspired by Spanish Surrealist Salvador Dalí and his painting *The Persistence of Memory*. If it is, the influences do not stop there.

Although Pioli produced a large number of guitars in his purpose-built, circular factory, and had a great reputation both in Italy and elsewhere, he chose to go out at the top. Pioli abandoned his lutherie around 1968 to make leather goods, and to devote himself to his art and to riding his motorcycle in the hills of Emilia-Romagna.

The sound of his guitars lives on at the hands of great guitarists, including Marc Ribot. Ribot's fluid, angular solo lines, and his complex expressionist chord patterns, are not just the work of a truly great guitarist; they seem especially suited to the Wandré. Find Ribot's great body of guitar work on his own albums, and recordings with Tom Waits and Elvis Costello.

Gibson
L-5 CES
1962

Type and body: Archtop electric jazz guitar.
Spruce top. Maple body and sides.
Neck and Fingerboard: Maple neck.
Ebony fingerboard.
Pickups: Two Gibson P-90 pickups.

Every so often a musician appears and changes the world. Wes Montgomery was just such a musician, and his guitar of choice was a 1962 Gibson L-5 CES.

Gibson first produced the L-5 in 1923, designed by Lloyd Loar, who was, at that time, the lead designer at Gibson. It was the first guitar ever to feature f-holes, at that time more commonly seen on violins, cellos, and basses. In its design and construction, the L-5 was of such a high quality that it quickly became the guitar of choice for jazz players of the 1920s. As big bands emerged at the end of the 1920s, the Gibson L-5 was always on the bandstand.

In the 1940s electric amplification became the craze, a way to make the guitar louder. It needed to be audible over the rhythm section of drums and bass, as well as the horn section, which could have as many as six or seven players blowing hard. With the addition of two P-90 pickups, Gibson introduced the CES model, the letters standing for *Cutaway, Electric, Spanish*. The cutaway was required because with amplification the frets at

the higher end of the fingerboard could actually be heard for the first time, allowing for players to exploit the dynamics and higher pitches of these top notes.

From 1958, the P-90s were replaced by humbuckers, and later in the 1960s, Montgomery played an L-5 with the original round Venetian cutaway. It is the later guitar that famously has a heart-shaped mother-of-pearl insert just below the strings, where Montgomery almost wore a hole where he rested his fingers while his thumb did all the picking and strumming.

Montgomery was completely self-taught as a musician and guitarist, practicing late into the night after completing a full day's work as a welder. Montgomery's inspiration was Charlie Christian, whom he heard play in his native Indianapolis. In 1948 Lionel Hampton heard Montgomery play and invited him to join his band. That was the beginning of a journey that would eventually find Montgomery fame as the greatest jazz guitarist of the mid-twentieth century, and one whose influence would be profound.

Because he never received any formal musical education, Montgomery never learned to use a plectrum, or pick, in his playing. Much has been written about Montgomery's use of his thumb to pick and strum his musical narrative line, and his use of octaves and complex chords. But this tells only half the story of this brilliant and sophisticated musician. For the other half, you have to listen to his music. Among his many recordings, listen to Montgomery's album *Movin' Wes*, on which you will hear him playing a 1962 Gibson L-5 CES. Listen to "Caravan" on the album, and you will not only hear Montgomery's wonderful playing, but you will hear the style that has influenced many of the greatest guitarists of the modern era, including George Benson and Pat Metheny.

The guitar pictured is a 1964 model.

Kay
K592 Red Devil
1962

Type and body: Double-cutaway, hollow-body electric guitar. Maple body.
Neck and Fingerboard: Mahogany neck. Rosewood fingerboard.
Pickups: Two Kay single-coil Speedbump pickups.

Kay Musical Instrument Company was founded in 1931, when Henry "Kay" Kuhrmeyer bought out his partners, Frank Voisinet and Charles Stromberg, from their eponymous company, Stromberg-Voisinet. The Chicago company had been successful during the 1920s, producing a stream of folk instruments, including mandolins, tenor guitars (four-string guitars), Hawaiian guitars, and banjos.

Part of Kay's success was its business building guitars that could be branded by the major mail-order companies, including Sears, Roebuck & Co. with its huge Silvertone line and Montgomery Ward with Airline. It wasn't until after World War II that Kay hit its stride with its own guitars, instruments that balanced excellent design and reasonably good quality with low price. The first, most famously successful, was the K161 Thin Twin, taken up and played by well-known bluesman Jimmy Reed. There followed a succession of decent, good-looking guitars, including the K592 Red Devil, which appeared in 1962.

Curiously, Kay (or Kraft, an in-house brand used to market the K592) didn't use the name Red Devil. That honor went to British importer Höhner, which likened the two sharp Venetian cutaways to the devil's horns. The marketing ploy worked, and the Red Devil became a popular budget electric guitar for British guitar fans.

The guitar itself was bedeviled by production problems, most notoriously the neck, which, when sloppily aligned, made the guitar all but unplayable. Set up correctly, however, and the guitar is accurate, forgiving, and fun to play. As a piece of midcentury design, the Kay Red Devil is a delight, with its beautiful maple veneer body covered in a red lacquer. With a mahogany neck, and a lovely bound rosewood fingerboard, with pick-shaped fret markers, the guitar oozes cool in a budget package.

Today, like many midcentury American guitars, the Kay Red Devil is receiving renewed attention for its striking good looks and period-sounding electronics. While very few of the original thin, and thin-sounding, pickups remain on these guitars, replaced over the years by better-sounding electronics, an original Red Devil remains a real prize for fans of vintage guitars.

Brian May
Red Special
1963

Type and body: Double-cutaway, solid-body electric guitar. Oak body. Mahogany veneer top and back.
Neck and Fingerboard: Mahogany neck. Painted oak fingerboard.
Pickups: Three Burns Tri-Sonic single-coil pickups.

A guitarist's sound is often ascribed to the player's favorite instrument—a series of Telecasters, say, or a fondness for Gibson Les Pauls. Unique to the world of rock music is Queen guitarist Brian May, who has played only one guitar virtually throughout his career, and on all his major recordings. That guitar is the Red Special, built by a teenage May and his father, Harold, over the course of two years, 1963 and 1964.

May's initial problem was that he couldn't afford a decent guitar. By the early 1960s, with American guitars now coming into Great Britain in numbers, prices were rising fast, and even the best of the budget brands, Höfner, was out of young May's reach. With the ingenuity and intelligence typical of a young man whose favorite school subjects were math and physics (May would much later earn a PhD in astrophysics), May and his father set about building a semi-hollow-body electric guitar from scratch. Various pieces of recycled oak and mahogany went into the making of the guitar, including an oak table and a mahogany mantelpiece that a neighbor planned to throw out.

Semi-hollow-body guitars, such as Les Paul's original Log or the great Gibson ES-335 with its solid maple center section, are less prone to the feedback typical of a fully hollow-body guitar. May loved some feedback, but he wanted to control it, and the guitar's body, along with electronics of his own design, would give him exactly the sound he was after.

Much has been written about the sound of the Red Special pickups: three Burns Tri-Sonics, two of which have been potted in epoxy resin by May himself, again to control feedback. The handmade bridge and vibrato tailpiece were also built by May and his father, with the tailpiece both ingenious and of a minimal beauty, the springs coming from motorcycle valve springs, and the rest plundered from parts of a bicycle saddlebag.

To finish it off in May's desired red, he and his father used several layers of a common British paint, Rustins Plastic Coating, with a gloriously large, shaped pickguard made of black Perspex, another common British hardware store plastic.

All this would be meaningless had the guitar been abandoned once May found success and had the means to buy any guitar of his choosing. Instead, the Red Special became an integral part of May's guitar sound and Queen's theatrically over-the-top rock appeal.

Mosrite Ventures Mark 1 1963

Type and body: Double-cutaway, solid-body electric guitar. Alder body.
Neck and Fingerboard: Maple neck. Rosewood fingerboard.
Pickups: Two Mosrite hand-wound single-coil pickups.

Semie Moseley was a gifted luthier who, at the height of his company's business, was employing more than one hundred workers, producing upward of one thousand guitars a month. Moseley was born in Arkansas and raised in Bakersfield, California, 100 miles (160 km) north of Los Angeles. His first apprenticeship was at Rickenbacker, under German luthier Roger Rossmeisl, while another mentor was Los Angeles custom guitar maker Paul Bigsby.

Moseley began building his own custom guitars while working for Rickenbacker. This side hustle did not go unnoticed, and he was promptly fired. Moseley's pastor, Reverend Ray Boatright, funded him in his own venture, joined by his brother Andy. By combining his own name, Moseley, with Boatright, Moseley came up with Mosrite, and production began in a small space in Bakersfield.

There was no doubting Moseley's skill, both as a craftsman and designer. Moseley's major breakthrough was in collaboration with music group the Ventures. This so-called Ventures guitar, complete with the Ventures logo on the ornately carved headstock, was a big success. It has been described as a "Stratocaster in reverse," which does not do it justice. True, the lower "horn" of the double cutaway is longer than the upper, however, there the comparison to the Stratocaster ends and other design antecedents emerge, Rickenbacker for one. Rossmeisl's influence can be seen in the fluid shape of the body and, of course, the glorious German carve, which was one of Rossmeisl's signatures. This carved flourish is around the ends of the guitar's body, where a gentle slope is carved away from the center of the body, giving the guitar a fluid, organic, almost female contour. Similarly, the one-piece pickguard has the line of a designer's hand, sure and lovely. With twin pickups and Moseley's own version of Paul Bigsby's vibrato arm, the guitar sounded rich and warm and was a delight to play. The final, and celebrated, flourish was the abstract *M* carved in the headstock, which carried the Ventures logo.

For the famous Custom guitar from 1980, now installed in the Smithsonian Institution in Washington, D.C., the design influence goes back to the greatest Los Angeles customizer, and Moseley's mentor, Bigsby. Moseley took the pillowy form of the Bigsby and enriched it with a luscious pickguard, cast metal components, and, best of all, an Italian violin scroll on the lower cutaway.

For all his brilliance, Moseley had a hard time in business, and Mosrite dwindled as he aged. Moseley's legacy is secure, however, not least because of customers as diverse as Elvis Presley, who owned a Mosrite, and more recently Johnny Ramone, who famously played a black-and-white Mosrite Ventures, leading it to become a favorite guitar of American punk players.

Airline/Valco Res-O-Glas 1964

Type and body: Semi-hollow-body electric guitar. Res-O-Glas resin–laminated body.
Neck and Fingerboard: Steel-reinforced maple neck. Rosewood fingerboard.
Pickups: Two single-coil pickups.

Airline was another of those budget American brands that made fabulous-looking, and often reasonably good-sounding, guitars. Airline was the in-house brand for Montgomery Ward, the biggest mail-order company in the United States, which supplied a variety of goods to people living in rural areas of the country who otherwise would not have had access to quality retail merchandise.

Montgomery Ward sourced its guitars from generic guitar makers, including Valco, which made the Res-O-Glas. The body design is unusual, a space-age cross between Gibson's Firebird and Explorer shapes. There the comparison ends. It was a cheap, and cheaply made, guitar, taking its name from the type of fiberglass-reinforced plastic that was used in its construction. The top and bottom were laid up in molds using the classic fiber-resin technique, with a colored gelcoat followed by reinforcing layers of fiber mixed with liquid resin. Once released from the molds, the two tops were joined together around a maple wood core to form a semi-hollow guitar body.

Two players have made the Res-O-Glas their signature guitar—one relatively unknown, the other famous. J. B. Hutto was an underappreciated blues singer and guitarist who, although born in the Deep South, in Blackville, South Carolina, moved with his family to Chicago. Hutto served in the Korean War, where he was a U.S. Army truck driver. Returning to Chicago, Hutto started building his career as a performer with a signature slide guitar and a punching blues voice. He chose the Res-O-Glas presumably because he couldn't afford a better guitar, but he made it his own, and it features on the cover of his *Sidewinder* album.

Jack White is an erudite musician with a deep knowledge of American pop culture, especially the blues. He knew J. B. Hutto's music well, and he was attracted to the raw, bluesy sound of Hutto's Res-O-Glas. He also liked the guitar because of its color—a bright lipstick red—and it became a signature of both his look and his sound during several years of his band the White Stripes. White's Res-O-Glas is now in the permanent music instrument collection of the Metropolitan Museum of Art in New York, an exalted resting place for such a humble guitar.

Jack White playing his red-on-red Res-O-Glas in 2003.

Rickenbacker 360/12 1964

Type and body: Double-cutaway, semi-hollow-body, twelve-string electric guitar. Maple body.
Neck and Fingerboard: Maple and walnut neck. Rosewood fingerboard.
Pickups: Two Rickenbacker single-coil Hi-Gain pickups.

California company Rickenbacker is one of the storied names of electric guitar making, and its following among the best guitarists over the course of almost one hundred years is an eloquent testament to the quality of its instruments.

The company was formed when inventor George Beauchamp and Swiss engineer Adolph Rickenbacker joined with Paul Barth with the expressed desire to manufacture playable electric guitars. With experience gained from building National guitars with the Dopyera brothers, the three created the Frying Pan, a lap steel Hawaiian guitar that is generally regarded as the first production electric guitar. The Frying Pan was only the beginning, however, and Rickenbacker quickly moved to make a broader range of quality guitars that were essentially lap steels with a wooden guitar-shaped body, sold as Electro guitars.

In 1953, Rickenbacker sold the company to well-known Los Angeles radio and PA manufacturer Francis C. Hall. Hall knew Leo Fender well, and he understood both the electronics of electric guitar making and the surge in popularity for rock and roll and pop music. Hall lured German luthier Roger Rossmeisl away from Gibson to bring top-class design and production ideas to Rickenbacker. Rossmeisl's designs were beautiful to look at and great to play. The design featured a distinctive, seductively curved double-cutaway body, with a slashed sound hole on the top of the body (the better to show that this was not an ordinary solid-body guitar), a lozenge pickguard that held the tone and volume controls, and a distinctive *R*-shaped tailpiece. To complete the look, the Rickenbacker name was emblazoned on the headstock.

By the late 1950s, Rickenbacker was exporting guitars to Europe, although not yet to Great Britain, which was restricting imports of goods from the United States. In Germany in 1960, a young John Lennon bought an early Model 325, which became his go-to guitar on stage and in the studio. Lennon's virtuoso fast-triplet rhythm part of "All My Loving" is played on the Rickenbacker Model 325. George Harrison quickly

followed suit, acquiring a prototype 360/12 directly from Francis Hall on the Beatles' first trip to New York City, and he put it to immediate use on many songs of the period, most notably "A Hard Day's Night." Roger McGuinn, the leader of California band the Byrds, saw Harrison playing the 360/12 in the movie *A Hard Day's Night* (1964) and decided that he had to have one. The joke is that George Harrison sold more 360/12s than any guitar dealer. If one of those "sales" was to McGuinn, together they continued to promote Rickenbacker guitars for many years to come.

The guitar pictured is a 1966 model.

Del Vecchio Dinâmico c.1965

Type and body: Acoustic resonator guitar.
Laminated rosewood body.
Neck and Fingerboard: Mahogany neck.
Rosewood fingerboard.

The Del Vecchio guitar company was founded in São Paulo, Brazil, in 1902 to make guitars and other stringed instruments, including the native cavaquinho and viola caipiras. By the 1930s, no doubt influenced by the guitars of George Beauchamp and John Dopyera at National, Del Vecchio started making resonator guitars. In the days before electronic amplification, the resonator was an acoustic solution to the continuing challenge of creating an instrument that could be heard above the crowd. The most famous of all Del Vecchios is the Dinâmico, which came in a purely acoustic form and, much later, with a single pickup. The Dinâmico has a single cone and as many as ten sound holes. Because Del Vecchio also made classical guitars, he used similar wide necks for his resonators, which joined the body at the twelfth fret. The bodies were generally made of Brazilian rosewood but in a cheaper, laminated form, presumably to keep the price of the guitars down.

There is no question that the Del Vecchio is one of the most beautiful guitars ever designed, with a sweet, slightly haunting, sustained sound.

On tour with Chet Atkins in the 1950s, the Brazilian brothers Antenor and Nato Lima gave Atkins a Del Vecchio, and he promptly recorded with it. Other guitarists to use the Dinâmico are Earl Klugh and Leo Kottke, and it was Klugh who persuaded Nashville luthier Paul McGill to build a guitar using the Del Vecchio design. McGill is now the preeminent maker of Dinâmico-style resonator guitars in the world. Look for vintage video of Chet Atkins and Nato Lima recorded by Paul McGill, and marvel at the sound of the guitar and the playing of Atkins and Lima.

Epiphone Casino 1965

Type and body: Double-cutaway, hollow-body electric guitar. Maple body.
Neck and Fingerboard: Mahogany neck. Rosewood fingerboard.
Pickups: Two P-90 pickups.

The screeching opening bars of the Beatles' "Revolution," released in 1968, could not have sounded as good on any other guitar. Nor, for that matter, the guitar licks and solo that punctuate "Get Back," released the following year. All these, and many more unmistakable guitar parts, are the work of John Lennon, on his "favorite guitar," the 1965 Epiphone Casino.

John Lennon, in an interview with *Rolling Stone*, said, "If George Harrison was the forgotten singer of the Beatles, then I was the forgotten guitar player." Hardly forgotten but sometimes underestimated. Lennon's use of the Epiphone Casino as his guitar is a testament to its quality and playability. Sweet and loud, the Epiphone Casino was a tangible bridge between jazz-leaning hollow-body guitar designs, including the ES guitars from Gibson, and the solid-body guitars that increasingly dominated rock music as the 1960s gave way to the 1970s, the punk era, and beyond.

The Epiphone Casino was introduced after Epiphone had been acquired by Gibson in 1957.

Gibson's plan was to produce budget-priced versions of their own more expensive models. The Casino is identical to the Gibson ES-330, which was introduced in 1959, while the Casino was introduced two years later, in 1961. The guitar is a hollow-body guitar design, with a double cutaway, two Gibson P-90 pickups, and a fixed, trapeze-style tailpiece. Many players added a Bigsby vibrato to their guitars. Lennon chose to keep his stock.

The Casino was something of a Beatles guitar. Paul got the first one in 1964, followed by George and John in 1965. While most Casinos came in a sunburst pattern, John had his sanded down to its laminated maple body, then lightly varnished, which gave the big guitar its signature natural blonde look. He also removed the pickguard.

One of the delights of Peter Jackson's Beatles documentary, *Get Back*, is seeing John, sitting down, comfortably knocking out chord after chord, lick after lick, while playing his Casino, whether working on a Beatles song or when the band would spontaneously erupt on one of many covers, perfectly played. At one point, John, sitting down, lofts his big Epiphone over his head, saying, "John entrusts his favorite guitar to . . ." and the moment ends.

Perhaps the most famous moment in the Epiphone Casino's life was on 30 January 1969, in London, when the Beatles, joined by Billy Preston on keyboards, played their famous rooftop concert. Arrayed across the rooftop, and captured on film and stills, were three of the greatest guitarists of all time: Paul playing his Höfner bass, George playing a newly gifted Rosewood Telecaster, and John playing his Epiphone Casino. It was the last time the Beatles played together live.

John Lennon with his one-off supergroup, The Dirty Mac, featuring Eric Clapton, Keith Richards, and Mitch Mitchell, in December 1968.

Guild
F-50
1965

Type and body: Steel-string acoustic guitar.
Spruce top. Maple body.
Neck and Fingerboard: Mahogany neck.
Rosewood fingerboard.

Founded in New York in 1952, Guild was the brainchild of music-store owner Alfred Donge, who took advantage of a long strike at Epiphone to poach some of its best craftsmen, including Henry Cappiello, "Little Louie" Cosco, and Frank Triggiani, expert luthiers in the great Italian tradition. Donge's idea was to make high-end guitars, and his small team of craftsmen got off to a quick start, making a range of electric guitars and archtops aimed squarely at jazz musicians. The guitars were good, they sold well, and demand grew. Guild was born.

As the 1960s folk boom spread from Greenwich Village in New York City, Guild's flattop acoustic guitars became among the best guitars available, on a par with anything available from Gibson or Martin, at a slightly better price. At the same time, some notable players, including Muddy Waters and Lovin' Spoonful lead guitarist Zal Yanovsky, took up the oddly shaped but great-sounding Thunderbird electric guitar, and these guitars were popular through the 1960s and 1970s.

At the 1969 Woodstock Music and Art Fair, Richie Havens, a Greenwich Village stalwart, played a riveting set on his Guild D-40. Guild was at its peak, and Guild's acoustic guitars were in heavy demand.

Bonnie Raitt is one of the very best guitarists of the late twentieth century, and she started on a Stella, a well-known acoustic guitar given to her by her musical parents. After dropping out of Harvard to pursue a full-time musical career, Raitt acquired a Guild F-50, which came to be closely identified with her acoustic style. And although Raitt is now known for her virtuoso Stratocaster slide guitar playing, it is the Guild F-50 that defines the sound of her earliest records. One of Raitt's first hits was "Angel from Montgomery," written by John Prine and recorded by Raitt in 1974. Look for Raitt and Prine singing "Angel from Montgomery" together, with Raitt playing her Guild F-50 with its characteristic double pickguard.

The model pictured is a F-50R with rosewood back and sides.

Rickenbacker Rose Morris 1993 1965

Type and body: Double-cutaway, semi-hollow-body twelve-string electric guitar. Maple body.
Neck and Fingerboard: Maple neck. Rosewood fingerboard.
Pickups: Two Rickenbacker single-coil pickups.

Tom Petty never met a Rickenbacker guitar that he didn't love, and this Rose Morris special is right up there with his favorite guitars of all.

Based on the Rickenbacker 360/12 twelve-string, the guitar is special in the sense that it came with some unique features requested by venerable London music store Rose Morris in Covent Garden, London, and Rickenbacker agents in England. One obvious change is the f-hole in the upper body. Where normal Rickenbackers would have a sound hole in the shape of a modernist, gestural slash, Rose Morris felt that European players would prefer the traditional f-hole.

Tom Petty loved the sound of a twelve-string electric guitar, just as his friends George Harrison and Roger McGuinn did. Harrison was first, playing a Rickenbacker 360/12 in the Beatles' 1964 movie *A Hard Day's Night*, a prototype given to him in New York City by the owner of Rickenbacker, F. C. Hall. McGuinn saw the movie with his bandmates in the Byrds, and they carefully noted the guitars the Beatles were using. McGuinn has said that when he realized Harrison was playing a twelve-string, he had to have one. Tom Petty's attraction to the Rickenbacker came much later but was just as deep. Petty was browsing his favorite Los Angeles guitar store, Norman's Rare Guitars, when he saw this guitar and took it to be a 360/12. Instead, it was this rare Rose Morris model, and he fell in love with it and used it extensively thereafter. Look for Tom Petty's halftime performance at the 2008 Super Bowl to hear exactly the jangly sound that this guitar is famous for, and this great guitarist loved.

Teisco Spectrum V 1966

Type and body: Double-cutaway, solid-body electric guitar. Mahogany body.
Neck and Fingerboard: Laminated ebony neck. Ebony fingerboard.
Pickups: Three Teisco split single-coil pickups.

The Japanese Teisco guitar company was founded in Tokyo in 1948 by Hawaiian guitarist Atsuwo Kaneko and electronic engineer Doryu Matsuda. It was not until the late 1950s, however, that their highly idiosyncratic designs were imported into Great Britain and the United States. Even then, Teisco guitars only flourished for a short number of years before the company was purchased by music instrument giant Kawai in 1967.

What set the Teisco guitars apart were their unusual shapes and their fantastic electronics. Teisco pickups were one good reason to buy the guitar. As a bonus, Teisco guitars came with as many as four pickups, with single tone and volume controls but intricate switching controls, giving the player wide latitude in experimenting with tone and sustain. To add to the appeal, the pickups were very good and are still coveted today; a thriving market for them exists on Internet auction sites. The body shapes were unusual, too, with the so-called "artist's palette" shape available on what was called the May Queen. Other shapes were more like the typical Fender lookalike, with a double cutaway and an elegant headstock with a little horn, on which was emblazoned either a badge or the Teisco name.

Among the best Teisco models, the Spectrum IV had everything a guitarist in search of an unusual-looking guitar with a great sound would want. Played through a decent amp, the Teisco can sound amazing in the right hands, belying its reputation as a cheap, idiosyncratic guitar made for strange guitarists.

Part of a loose coalition of well-respected California musicians including Ry Cooder, Jackson Browne, Bonnie Raitt, Graham Nash, and David Crosby, David Lindley has been described not as a multi-instrumentalist but a maxi-instrumentalist. Among the many guitars that Lindley has played and recorded with are several Teiscos, including a Spectrum IV. Lindley's debut album with his own band, *El Rayo-X*, was released in 1981 and is an excellent introduction to Lindley's musical brilliance and technical prowess.

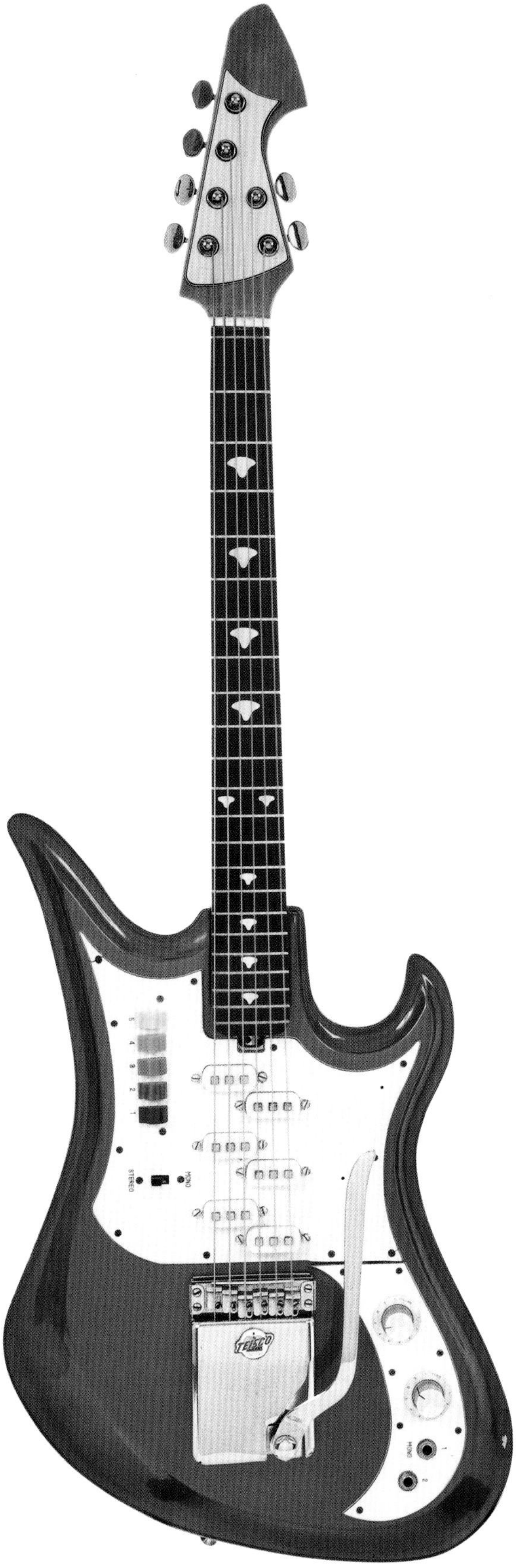
STEREO
MONO
MONO

Fender Stratocaster 1968

Type and body: Double-cutaway, solid-body electric guitar. Alder body.
Neck and Fingerboard: Maple neck. Maple fingerboard.
Pickups: Three single-coil pickups.

When Leo Fender and Freddie Tavares were working on their guitars and Tavares sketched the shape of the Stratocaster, little could they have known the impact it would have on the world of popular music. The Stratocaster is simply the most famous, most important guitar ever designed. This guitar, serial number 240981—a standard Stratocaster in Olympic White—is perhaps the most famous Strat of all. Owned and played by Jimi Hendrix at the Woodstock Music and Art Fair, the guitar redefines the idea of cool. Countless guitar players, treating themselves to a custom Stratocaster, have asked for exactly this configuration.

Jimmy Hendrix (he hadn't changed the spelling yet) was working with the Isley Brothers, playing an Isley-owned Stratocaster, and living in the family home in New Jersey. When he told them he was leaving the band, they asked him if he had a guitar. When Hendrix said he didn't, they gave him the Strat he had been playing with the band, and he left. Hendrix eventually ended up in London, where he found an enthusiastic, receptive audience for his guitar playing, his singing, and the utterly new sound of his band, the Jimi Hendrix Experience. The Beatles went to see him in the small London club that he played on weeknights. And in June 1967, three days after their new album was released, the Beatles saw Hendrix open a show with his version of the title track, "Sgt. Pepper's Lonely Hearts Club Band," during which his improvisatory playing and string-bending left his Stratocaster completely out of tune. Performances such as this, and his era-defining performances at both Woodstock in 1969, where he played this guitar, and the Isle of Wight in 1970, combined to form the wide appreciation of Hendrix as the greatest rock guitarist of his era, if not of all time.

Like many of the great blues musicians before him, Jimi Hendrix's music came from another place—from the existential pain of Black American heritage, from the desolation of poverty, from the irreplaceable loss of an absent mother and an uncaring, and possibly worse, father. It came from Jimi's own deep intelligence, his generosity, and, of course, from his ability to create sounds that had never before been dreamed of, let alone heard. Although Hendrix played other guitars, including a Supro and a Danelectro, his two first electric guitars, he liked standard Stratocasters purchased from guitar stores. Because he played left-handed, Hendrix would reverse the bridge on his guitars so that he could string them in reverse, but this was the only change he made to his instruments.

After his accidental death in London in September 1970, Jimi Hendrix's Stratocaster was all but forgotten, remaining in its case in the home of Experience drummer Mitch Mitchell. The guitar was eventually acquired by the Experience Music Project, the Seattle music museum, itself an homage to Seattle-born Hendrix. Now called MoPOP, the museum houses this Jimi Hendrix Stratocaster on permanent display.

Jimi Hendrix playing his favorite Olympic White Strat in 1969.

Vox
Mark VI
1968

Type and body: Teardrop, solid-body electric guitar. Ash body.
Neck and Fingerboard: Maple neck. Rosewood fingerboard.
Pickups: Three single-coil pickups.

Founded in England just after World War II, Vox established its reputation with a series of amplifiers that came to define the British rock sound of the 1950s. Because Vox amps were used by all the best bands, company founder Tom Jennings got to know the music business and the musicians well. Fender, Gibson, and other American guitars were difficult and expensive to buy in late-1950s Great Britain, so Jennings decided to make high-quality electric guitars under the Vox brand.

One of Vox's earliest efforts was the Apache, a lozenge-shaped guitar with a Fender-style maple neck, a beech fingerboard, three Vox pickups, and Vox's own vibrato bridge, which came to be known as the Hank Marvin bridge after the lead guitarist of the Shadows.

Emboldened by its success, in 1962 Jennings created the Phantom with an odd "coffin" shape, designed in collaboration with the London Design Centre. As ungainly as it looked, the guitar had an acceptable sound, was played by bands such as the Kinks and the Hollies, and sold well.

Ever inventive, Jennings created a prototype of a teardrop-shaped guitar in 1963 for Brian Jones of the Rolling Stones, using the Hank Marvin vibrato bridge but with only two pickups instead of the usual three. Going into production, Jennings reverted to the same three-pickup idea as the Stratocaster, redesigned the neck with an adjustable truss rod, kept the vibrato bridge, and called the guitar the Mark VI. Helped by the endorsement of such a cool guitar player as Brian Jones, the guitar's radical design shape somehow captured the vibe of swinging sixties London to perfection and became a big success.

The teardrop shape, the overall build quality, and the excellent electronics of the Mark VI proved a good starting point for several offshoots, including a twelve-string electric and a hollow-body bass, endorsed by another Rolling Stones player, Bill Wyman.

Not only because of the teardrop Mark VI but also because of Vox's line of outstanding amps, the Vox name is as important to British pop and rock history as the Beatles, the Hollies, the Kinks, and the Rolling Stones.

Martin N-20 Trigger 1969

Type and body: Classical acoustic guitar.
Spruce top. Brazilian rosewood back and sides.
Neck and Fingerboard: Mahogany neck.
Ebony fingerboard.
Pickups: One Baldwin Prismatone pickup.

Martin guitars are steel-string instruments that more or less define the shape and sound of an American acoustic guitar. By the end of the 1960s, however, the folk boom had encouraged people to learn how to play the guitar, and Martin decided it needed a nylon-string, Spanish-style instrument to serve the classical sector of the market.

It was a handsome design for a classical Spanish guitar, with a manageable 25⅜-inch (64-cm) string scale, a classical rosette adorning the sound hole, and the characteristic square headstock of all Martins. It was a development of the so-called New York folk guitars of the early 1960s, which, although they looked like classical guitars, were designed and braced for steel strings. Made with expensive tone woods, including a spruce top, a beautiful Brazilian rosewood body, a mahogany neck, and an ebony fingerboard, the N-20 was not an entry-level guitar. Later models in the *N* series would have a longer neck and an ornate, Spanish-style peghead, but it didn't make any difference to sales, which were lackluster to begin with and petered out in the mid-1970s. It seems that the classical fans just could not imagine a Martin Spanish guitar.

Sometime in 1969, Willie Nelson's acoustic Baldwin, fitted with a Prismatone acoustic bridge pickup, was broken after a concert. Nelson sent the guitar to Nashville luthier Shot Jackson, who decided the guitar could not be fixed. He offered Nelson a new Martin N-20 for $750, and Nelson agreed, as long as his Prismatone pickup was salvaged from the Baldwin and fitted to the bridge of the Martin. The deal was done, and Jackson shipped the new guitar to Nelson.

Thus was born one of the most recognizable guitars in musical history. Nelson loved the sight and sound of his new guitar, eventually giving it the nickname Trigger after Roy Rogers's horse! As a classical guitar, it didn't have, nor would it have needed, a pickguard. But Nelson plays with a pick, and eventually he wore a huge hole in the spruce top, just below the sound hole. Since it didn't affect the tone of the guitar, Nelson has allowed the hole to stay—indeed to grow—in the intervening fifty-plus years on the road.

The sound of this Martin N-20 is now inseparable from Willie Nelson's voice and songs. It is as if the guitar was destined to be owned and played by Nelson, and it has a tone and sustain that are both luscious and unusual in country music. Nelson is a greatly underrated guitarist, playing his eccentric Martin with subtlety and nuance, and with solos in a style that is reminiscent of Django Reinhardt, one of Nelson's guitar heroes.

Giannini
CRA6S Craviola
1970

Type and body: Single-cutaway acoustic guitar.
Sitka spruce top. Rosewood back and sides.
Neck and Fingerboard: Mahogany neck.
Rosewood fingerboard.

Best known as a composer and singer, Brazilian guitarist Paulinho Nogueira should also be celebrated as a brilliant designer, whose Craviola is one of the most distinctive and beautiful guitar designs ever made. Its sound is distinctive, a cross between a harpsichord (in Portuguese, *cravo*) and the traditional ten-string Brazilian guitar, the viola caipira. Nogueira coined the name Craviola for his creation and collaborated with São Paulo instrument maker Giorgio Giannini to produce the guitar.

It was produced in three styles, including a twelve-string. Although it has been played by notable players, including Jimmy Page, who played a twelve-string Craviola, it has been largely ignored. This is a shame, given the distinctive and beautiful sound it creates.

The body shape echoes that of a lute—a large teardrop shape on the upper body, disrupted by the flowing, wavelike lower body. This disruption of the traditional acoustic guitar shape has its detractors, but it is hard to argue with the sound: bell-like, sweet, with a lovely sustain. The D-shaped sound hole is reminiscent of Mario Maccaferri's Selmer, the mustache bridge harkens back to nineteenth-century Italy, and the generous neck has all the feel of a classical guitar. The guitar's materials are traditional: Sitka spruce top with laminated rosewood sides and back, a mahogany neck, and a rosewood fingerboard. With a characteristic flourish, Nogueira gave the headstock a little comma shape, almost a wink.

Largely ignored by guitar aficionados, perhaps the time is now right for a reappraisal of this elegant and sweet-sounding acoustic guitar.

Ovation Breadwinner 1974

Type and body: Single-cutaway, solid-body electric guitar. Ovation Lyrachord resin-painted mahogany.
Neck and Fingerboard: Maple neck. Ebony fingerboard.
Pickups: Active toroidal single-coil pickups.

Seismic shifts are rare in the world of guitar design. The classical guitar evolved at the hands of master luthiers in Italy, Germany, and Spain. The acoustic guitar as we know it was the work of C. F. Martin and, later, Orville Gibson. Leo Fender, Paul Bigsby, and Les Paul all contributed to major movements in the paradigm of wood, wire, and metal. Add to that august list aeronautical engineer and polymath Charles Kaman, who, through meticulous research and a florid scientific imagination, found new directions in both acoustic guitar and electric guitar design.

Kaman's first work was in aeronautics, working for Igor Sikorsky on helicopter design before starting his own aviation company at the end of World War II. In his spare time, Kaman was a guitar lover and collector, and he constantly toyed with ideas for the construction of acoustic guitars, using the kind of space-age materials familiar to him in his work in aeronautics. In 1966 Kaman founded what would become the Ovation Guitar Company to produce his signature acoustic guitar, which has a lutelike round composite back.

Charles Kaman's acoustic guitar was such a success that it was inevitable that he and his engineers would turn their attention to the solid-body electric guitar, a realm long dominated by Gibson and Fender. Almost as a preparation, Kaman and his engineer, James Rickard, made innovations with piezo bridge pickups on his acoustic guitars. When it came to electric guitars, Ovation started with semi-solid-body designs before settling on a series of solid-body instruments known as Breadwinners.

The first thing to notice is the ax shape of the guitar body, a visual pun on the popular nickname for an electric guitar: ax. It was also claimed by Ovation to be an ergonomic design, not something that electric guitar makers have been known for through the decades. The body was interesting for another reason, too: a solid mahogany block, covered by Ovation's patented laminated plastic—Lyrachord—which was certainly durable. With a beautiful ebony fingerboard, a maple neck, and the characteristic lyre-shaped headstock, this was clearly an elegant, high-end guitar, designed to be taken seriously.

The Breadwinner's active electronics meant that the built-in preamp and the switching, along with Ovation's own toroidal pickups (later replaced by humbuckers), allowed the player to explore a wide range of settings and tones.

As successful as Ovation's acoustic guitars were, and despite typically good Ovation electronics in their electric guitars, the Breadwinner was, perhaps unfairly, shunned by the guitar-buying public and disappeared from production in the early 1980s.

Travis Bean TB500 1976

Type and body: Solid-body electric guitar. Koa body.
Neck and Fingerboard: Aluminum neck. Brazilian rosewood fingerboard.
Pickups: Three single-coil pickups.

Travis Bean set up his guitar-making business in California in 1974 to make electric guitars and basses featuring a one-piece aluminum neck. Aluminum necks were not new, of course, but Bean and fellow luthiers Marc McElwee and Gary Kramer wanted to create new, high-end guitars that would look, feel, and sound different from the Gibsons and Fenders then dominating rock music.

The real innovation in the Bean designs was the way the one-piece neck extended into the body, reminiscent of Les Paul's wooden four-by-four "Log" from over thirty years earlier. Bean machined his neck with a stunning *T* cutout in the headstock, both becoming a trademark and suggesting a see-through lightness. As Les Paul had done with his wooden Log, Bean extending the neck into the body allowed him to attach pickups of his own design as well as the tailpiece, also a Bean innovation. The bodies were typically made of koa wood and were beautifully shaped with soft and luxurious lines in a traditional, double-cutaway style, with a Brazilian rosewood fingerboard completing the high-end, custom guitar style.

The guitars sounded great and for a short while were highly desirable by players, including Keith Richards and Jerry Garcia. The knock on the designs was that they were just too heavy, especially in a concert setting. Kramer took note of the criticisms, left Bean, and set up his own shop, making aluminum-necked electric guitars with considerable success.

Travis Bean struggled on until shutting down in 1979, by which time he had produced more than 3,500 guitars and basses. As with many innovations not fully appreciated at the time of their making, vintage Travis Bean instruments are now eagerly collected by discerning guitar aficionados.

Ibanez
GB10
1977

Type and body: Single-cutaway, hollow-body electric guitar. Spruce top. Maple body.
Neck and Fingerboard: Maple neck. Ebony fingerboard.
Pickups: Two humbucker pickups.

Named for an early twentieth-century Spanish luthier, Salvador Ibáñez, the Japanese brand Ibanez was founded in 1908 but only came to international prominence in the late 1950s with a series of budget acoustic and electric guitars. This success continued during the 1960s, with a range of Fender and Gibson copies, before Ibanez started to produce a large range of its own designs, including electric, acoustic, and bass guitars.

By the mid-1970s, jazz guitarist George Benson was at the height of his crossover fame, and not just widely known and respected as a player but also as a great singer. Benson's playing in increasingly larger venues demanded a guitar that was less prone to feedback at high volumes than the Gibson jazz guitars that he typically played. Benson also wanted a lighter guitar, and he turned to Ibanez for help.

Jeff Hasselberg was chief designer for the U.S. division of Hoshino Gakki, parent company of Ibanez, and he began experimenting with thin-line, hollow-body shapes that would work for

Benson. Hasselberg sketched the body shapes of a Gibson Les Paul and a Gibson Johnny Smith archtop, and the result was the small, thin-line, hollow-body Ibanez GB10. George Benson was very happy with the guitar, and Ibanez released it in 1977 to considerable acclaim. Made of top-quality materials, the GB10 has a spruce top with two f-holes, tightly braced maple back and sides, maple neck, and ebony fingerboard. In another strategy to reduce feedback, the GB10 has two Ibanez humbucker pickups that float above the body, a small pickguard, an adjustable bridge, and an organically shaped split tailpiece that is adjustable, allowing for the strings to be fine-tuned to the player's preference.

Shortly after the release of the GB10, Joni Mitchell was preparing her jazz-inflected album *Mingus*, a collaboration with virtuoso jazz bassist Charles Mingus. Mitchell had generally played a Martin D-28 guitar over the course of her long career, but she now saw that the Ibanez GB10 was a suitably jazz-sounding guitar for her new material. Its light weight also appealed to her, especially because she was embarking on a tour in support of the *Mingus* album.

For that tour, Mitchell chose a band including Pat Metheny playing his Gibson ES-175 and Jaco Pastorius playing his unique Fender fretless jazz bass. Mitchell's use of complex chord voicings and subtle rhythms was perfectly suited to the Ibanez George Benson guitar, and resulted in a remarkable live album, *Shadows and Light*. The *Shadows and Light* concert, filmed at the Santa Barbara Bowl in September 1979, includes Mitchell's stunning "Amelia," immediately followed by Metheny's "Pat's Solo." In these two pieces, we see and hear two of the greatest musicians of the modern era at their astonishing best.

Joni Mitchell playing one of her GB10s, originally purchased for her 1979 *Mingus* album.

Ovation Adamas 1977

Type and body: Hollow-body acoustic guitar. Lyrachord resin body shell. Composite-laminated birch top.
Neck and Fingerboard: Maple neck. Rosewood fingerboard.
Pickups: Piezo electronic bridge pickup.

Ovation founder Charles Kaman was an aeronautical engineer, an industrialist, and a successful entrepreneur. However, it was in his lifelong love of the guitar that he made a big impact on popular culture. Always looking for ways to improve existing designs, and having access to a team of accomplished engineers and designers in his aeronautics factory, Kaman saw an opportunity to improve both the acoustic properties of the acoustic guitar and how it was built.

From the time of Stradivari, acoustic guitars have been made by using labor-intensive carpentry to shape and form the tops and bottoms and then gluing everything together to the sides before fitting the neck, the fingerboard, and other parts. However, Kaman and his engineers hit on the idea of molding the back of the guitar in a shape much like a tortoise. In fact, it is like the shape of a mandolin or lute but made in one molded piece of what Kaman called Lyrachord, a resin-infused fabric similar to fiberglass. It was typical of Kaman and his engineers that they would reach into their aeronautical engineering practice to find a material that was strong, light, had good acoustic qualities, and was easy to fabricate.

Having decided on a molded back, Kaman then decided to make the guitar top in a similar composite material to eliminate wood completely from the guitar body. All this innovation was not simply for its own sake. It enabled a high-quality instrument to be made in an industrial process, and Kaman was very alert to the need to make his guitars look great, too. The body shapes, the variety of colors, the floral Art Deco sound holes, and the cutaway on some models all have a refinement, a fineness of line, that is evidence of the hands of truly great designers.

If the buying public, raised on traditional Martins and Gibsons, was a little slow to embrace this innovation, musicians saw the advantages of lightness combined with a great sound, and the guitar proved to be a long-term success for Ovation. With a piezo electronic pickup built into the bridge, the guitar could be plugged directly into an amplifier, giving the performer further flexibility in how the guitar's sound could be projected.

Among the first guitarist to showcase the Ovation was Anglo-Caribbean singer/songwriter Joan Armatrading, who recorded almost all her albums on Ovation acoustics, both six-string and twelve-string. "Willow" and "Woncha Come On Home," from Armatrading's 1977 album *Show Some Emotion,* capture this brilliant guitarist's Ovation playing. Keen listeners will also hear Georgie Fame's fantastic keyboard playing on the same album.

Kaki King is a guitarist whose playing, pulsing and percussive, seems perfectly matched to the strong, even-toned Ovation Adamas. Listen to King's album *Live at Berklee* to get a real feel for this marvelous musician's unique guitar style and wonderful singing of her beautifully crafted songs.

Eddie Van Halen Frankenstrat 1977

Type and body: Double-cutaway, solid-body electric guitar. Ash body.
Neck and Fingerboard: Maple neck. Maple fingerboard.
Pickups: One humbucker pickup.

Sometimes it is just not possible to imagine a guitar without thinking of the guitarist wielding it. Such is the case with Eddie Van Halen and his Frankenstrat, an instrument of Van Halen's own making. Of course, Eddie Van Halen did not literally make his guitar; instead, he assembled a collection of parts, which he changed many times over the years to achieve the sound and feel that he admired from both his Gibson ES-335 and a typical Fender Stratocaster.

There is some dispute about the neck and body, which Van Halen bought from Boogie Bodies, a supplier of one-off necks and bodies near Seattle. Who knows what they were, or if it even matters. What matters is that Eddie Van Halen assembled them, along with an assortment of other odd parts. The first vibrato system Van Halen used was from his own 1958 Stratocaster. He replaced this with a Floyd Rose vibrato system, or as Floyd Rose calls it, a tremolo.

Further "refinements" included a Gibson PAF pickup in the bridge position, which Van Halen eventually replaced with a Seymour Duncan humbucker. With his limited ability with wiring, Van Halen removed the tone and volume controls (known as "pots" for potentiometers) and replaced them with a simple volume control. In doing so, he apparently reduced his guitar's output to one pickup. Not bothered, Van Halen then covered up the wiring with a pickguard that he fabricated by breaking apart a vinyl LP.

In a final aesthetic flourish, Van Halen applied masking tape to the body at a variety of angles and, in a series of overlays, painted his guitar black, red, and white.

So much for the actual guitar, which received design validation when chosen by New York's Metropolitan Museum of Art for its "Play It Loud: Instruments of Rock & Roll" exhibition.

From Van Halen's vast oeuvre, one of his greatest solos was for a guest appearance on Michael Jackson's song "Beat It," commissioned by producer Quincy Jones, engineer Rod Temperton, and Jackson himself. Given indescribable energy by a mere thirty seconds of Van Halen's playing and the sound of his "parts bin special" guitar, the song was a huge and important hit for Jackson.

Collings #29 1978

Type and body: Flattop Dreadnought acoustic guitar. German spruce top. Indian rosewood back and sides.
Neck and Fingerboard: Maple neck. Ebony fingerboard.

Bill Collings is invariably described as a "medical school dropout," which is not quite true (he got as far as premed). From a family of practical engineers, and ever the tinkerer, Bill found premed boring and chose not to continue, preferring to build guitars, which he did on his kitchen table in Houston in the early 1970s.

Collings had a simple mission: to take the basic Martin and Gibson Dreadnought shapes and make them better. Lyle Lovett met Collings in 1978 and remembers him saying, "The thing is, you have your Martins and you have your Gibsons, and that's it." Lovett was so impressed by Collings and his lutherie skills that he ordered a guitar, receiving a delivery of a Martin-style Dreadnought in 1978. The new guitar did not have a style number—a D-this or an F-that. Nor did it have a Collings logo on the headstock. It was simply the twenty-ninth guitar that Collings had made and has been known as #29 ever since. It is arguably the guitar that put Collings on the map, because it coincided with the start of Lovett's stellar career and became a guitar that was widely seen and heard.

Guitarists say of Martins that while the middle strings are loud and bright, the top two strings are comparatively quiet. Collings knew this and worked to make sure that all strings on his guitars would be even in tone. With that mission, Collings built Gibson-style guitars with the characteristic sunburst finish and Martin-style guitars with a natural finish.

The guitar known as #29 has a German spruce top and Indian rosewood back and sides, the classic Martin herringbone binding, maple neck, ebony fingerboard, and an abalone rosette. It is not only a gorgeous-sounding acoustic guitar; it's an instrument of great beauty. Collings guitars typically have sharp-cornered headstocks, but the headstock on Lovett's guitar is softly rounded, like that of a Martin, without the logo.

Since those first guitars made on Bill Collings's kitchen table, Collings guitar production has grown both in reputation and size, and the Collings factory in Austin, Texas, now produces a full range of superb acoustic and electric guitars, mandolins, and ukuleles.

Multi-Grammy winner, actor, singer/songwriter, and guitarist, Lovett's career began with his eponymous album, *Lyle Lovett*, released in 1986. Lovett used his Collings #29 extensively on that album, and on many of the subsequent fourteen albums that he has released. Lovett's brilliant guitar playing can be heard on the opening arpeggios of one of his most famous songs, "If I Had a Boat," from the 1987 album *Pontiac*, played on his Collings, while his use of complex, jazz-inflected chord progressions can be heard on his hit song "She's No Lady," also from *Pontiac*.

Ibanez
AR500
1979

Type and body: Double-cutaway, solid-body guitar. Arched maple top. Mahogany body.
Neck and Fingerboard: Three-piece maple neck. Ebony fingerboard.
Pickups: Two Ibanez humbucker pickups.

From the outset, Ibanez wanted to make high-quality guitars, and to make a lot of them. Indeed, the name Ibanez itself was taken from the great turn-of-the-century Valencia luthier Salvador Ibáñez, whose instruments were admired and played all over the world, including in Japan. That parent company Hoshino Gakki appropriated the Ibáñez name (dropping the accents) to create an entirely new brand did not seem to cause them a moment's pause, which is why they got into trouble when they started producing electric guitars in the 1970s. In an inauspicious start to their electric ambitions, Ibanez copied Fender- and Gibson-style electric guitars so brazenly that they were immediately sued by both Fender and Gibson. Those early guitars would become known as the "lawsuit guitars." All that stopped in the late 1970s, when Ibanez began its growth into the giant it is today, both in the number and range of guitars it makes but also in the consistently high quality of those instruments.

The first electric guitars to make their mark were the Artist, Iceman, and Professional series, which were seen as high-quality alternatives to Fender and Gibson at a better price. The Artist series was vaguely Gibson SG-like, with twin cutaways, two good pickups, and an adjustable bridge but with more options on the controls. Unique design accents included a beautifully shaped tailpiece anchored to the body itself. It all made one wish for even more from the excellent production designers at Ibanez in Japan and their American agent, Hoshino, whose influence on everything that emerged from the many Ibanez factories was profound.

Steve Miller is an outstanding guitarist whose early adoption of Ibanez Artist and Iceman guitars was a key to their subsequent success. Often unfairly seen as a pop musician, Miller's musicianship comes from the deepest roots. Miller's pathologist father was a polymath, and a noted recording engineer, whose close friends included Les Paul, who was Steve Miller's godfather, and T-Bone Walker, who gave the young Miller guitar lessons.

Miller's playing on the Steve Miller Band's 1976 album *Fly Like An Eagle* is typical of his great guitar playing and musicianship and is perhaps his best, most enduring, recorded legacy.

Jackson
RR1
1981

Type and body: Solid-body electric guitar.
Maple body.
Neck and Fingerboard: Maple neck. Ebony
fingerboard.
Pickups: Two Seymour Duncan humbucker
pickups.

Luthier Grover Jackson took over the ailing
California guitar company Charvel in 1978 and
immediately made a mark with interesting electric guitars. Jackson's designs attracted, among
others, metal and hard-rock players, always on
the lookout for a visual signature, from big hair to
impossibly tight jeans to unusual guitars, anything
that might set them apart from the crowd.

Randy Rhoads was a classically trained electric
guitar virtuoso who asked Jackson to make a
guitar for him, and it was this commission that
launched Jackson Guitars.

During the 1970s, Rhoads was making his mark
with Quiet Riot, the band he formed with his
best friend, Kelly Garni. Their genre was hard
rock, soon to morph into heavy metal, and as
the guitarist, Rhoads quickly found fame both at
home in Los Angeles and further afield. By this
time, Rhoads needed a guitar to match his growing fame and he turned to Jackson, who took the
ideas that Rhoads brought and translated them
into four evolving Randy Rhoads specials. All

featured Rhoads's desired Flying V body shape
with top-of-the-line electronics and hardware.
Jackson brought his own design prowess to bear
on Rhoads's wishes, and the result was the Jackson
RR1. Rhoads had Jackson modify the body shape
into what became his preferred guitar shape,
an extended Flying V with the same high-end
equipment, which Rhoads called the Concorde.
Two more prototypes were in construction when,
in 1982, Rhoads was killed when the light aircraft
in which he was a passenger crashed during a
reckless maneuver performed by Ozzy Osbourne's
bus driver, who was flying the plane. Rhoads was
twenty-five years old.

That Rhoads was a brilliant musician came as no
surprise to his family and friends. Raised by a single
mother who was herself a gifted musician, Rhoads
was something of a prodigy and taught guitar at his
mother's North Hollywood music school, Musonia.
Guitar teacher by day, guitar shredder by night,
Rhoads and his band developed a friendly, if intense,
rivalry with Eddie Van Halen and his band. Before
long Rhoads was a major figure, and after a comical
audition process involving a drunk Ozzy Osbourne,
Rhoads eventually joined Osbourne's band.

Rhoads's understanding of classical scales, complex chord voicings, and unusual key signatures
gave the Osbourne band a guitar sophistication
that had rarely been heard on a heavy metal stage.
It is not an exaggeration to say that Rhoads's
virtuosity was lost on the limited musical genre
that is heavy metal. Because of his death, Rhoads's
potential as one of the great rock guitarists of his
generation was never fully realized.

José Luis Romanillos Vega La Lechuza 1981

Type and body: Classical acoustic guitar. Spruce top. Indian rosewood back and sides.
Neck and Fingerboard: Cedar neck. Ebony fingerboard.

The DNA of the classical guitar runs back several centuries to luthiers such as Belchior Dias, who worked in Lisbon, Portugal, in the late 1500s, and to Antonio Stradivari, who flourished fifty years later in Cremona, Italy. José Luis Romanillos Vega, born in Madrid in 1932, is one of those luthiers who brought the art and craft of classical guitar making forward in great strides while retaining all the outward appearances of an instrument made one hundred years earlier. It was not until around 1960 that Romanillos, a cabinetmaker in the grand Spanish tradition, made his first guitar. His first efforts were good, and a meeting with the great English guitarist Julian Bream spurred Romanillos into full-time work making classical guitars with the best woods and the best hardware that he could make or find.

All guitar makers look for balance in their strings, whether this is a balance of harmonics and color or a simple balance of volume from each of the six strings. Purity of tone is the holy grail, and with the great work coming from his Wiltshire studio, Romanillos garnered a big reputation for beautiful guitars that were pure in balance, tone, and volume. This quest is key to understand the challenges facing the maker of modern classical guitars. The instruments have to have greater volume and sustain than their antique counterparts, and have to have perfect balance. Of his work, Romanillos has this to say: "I am trying to make an instrument that is as intimate . . . and as beautiful as I can. With a small guitar, the sound is more in focus. With a larger guitar, you seem to be further away from it."

The relationship between Bream and Romanillos was important to both men, and the result of their collaboration is this guitar, made for Bream in 1981. Romanillos nicknamed it La Lechuza (the Owl) because he sensed the look and feel of an owl's wisdom in the finished guitar. The tone of the guitar has been widely acclaimed, both from the softest top notes, which have been described as crystalline, to the loudest bass notes, which are filled with strength and depth. In addition, all of the notes, at every volume, have the long sustain craved by modern classical virtuosos.

With a spruce top and luscious Indian rosewood sides and back, the guitar features some characteristic Romanillos flourishes, including abstract arch shapes in the rosette inspired by the arches of the great mosque in Córdoba, Spain. Bream played La Lechuza for many years, a testament to the beauty of its making.

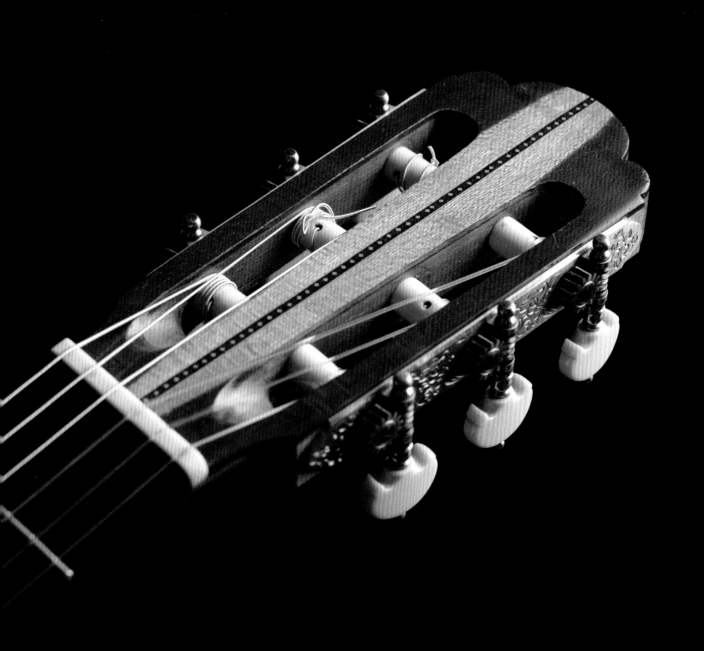

Hohner
HG490
1983

Type and body: Solid-body electric guitar.
Ash body.
Neck and Fingerboard: Maple neck.
Maple fingerboard.
Pickups: Two single-coil pickups.

We know from history that many great guitarists played basic, inexpensive instruments either because in their youth they couldn't afford anything better or, as in the case of British guitarists in the 1950s and early 1960s, including the Beatles, quality guitars were simply not available. George Harrison played an Egmond Toledo Rosetti. And Jimmy Page played a Resonet Grazioso Futurama, made to look like a Stratocaster. Jimi Hendrix's first guitar was a Supro Ozark. Cheap guitars each one.

And then there are the unusual musicians who prefer to play run-of-the-mill, inexpensive guitars. Prince was one of those, whose devotion to his Hohner HG490 was charming and lasted almost four decades before Prince's untimely death in 2016.

Prince's Hohner was made to look like a Fender Telecaster, with its signature horizontal control plate on the lower body. It had a cool pickguard that was more leopard skin than tortoiseshell, a pair of single-coil pickups, and that was it. The rest of the guitar was as you would expect from an inexpensive instrument. There was no finesse to it until the moment Prince picked it up, plugged it in, and unleashed his genius on its six strings.

Although Prince has often been described as a multi-instrumentalist, in the years since his passing, his recognition as one of the great rock virtuoso guitarists has grown, and deservedly so. Whether it is his incredibly subtle rhythm licks on a track such as Stevie Wonder's "So What the Fuss" or full-on rock shredding, as on his own "Let's Go Crazy," his playing is always perfectly integrated into the song, and it is always great.

Perhaps the best example of Prince's guitar prowess was his performance on "While My Guitar Gently Weeps" in 2004 for George Harrison at the Rock and Roll Hall of Fame. After the rest of the all-star band had taken their turn, Prince played a solo that was the epitome of rock guitar virtuosity. At the end of his solo, in a typical gesture, Prince threw his beloved Hohner high into the air, as if he was going to throw it into the audience. As he turned to strut offstage, he glanced over his shoulder to make sure his guitar-tech had caught his beloved, priceless, cheap Hohner HG490 Telecaster-lookalike guitar. It was a perfect Prince moment in every way.

Prince made this humble Hohner guitar famous.

James L. D'Aquisto
Avant Garde
1988

Type and body: Archtop acoustic guitar.
Spruce top. Maple body.
Neck and Fingerboard: Maple neck.
Ebony fingerboard.

The tradition of Italian immigrant luthiers working in and around New York City goes to the heart of American guitar production in the twentieth century. James L. D'Aquisto was born in Brooklyn in 1935, the son of first-generation Italian parents, and he had a zeal for everything he did, especially for the spectacular archtop guitars that came from his hands.

As a teenager, and growing up in a musical family, D'Aquisto was a jazz fanatic and an enthusiastic jazz guitar player. At that time, John D'Angelico was the greatest archtop luthier. It was natural that D'Aquisto would know and admire the older man's work. D'Aquisto visited D'Angelico's workshop as a sixteen year old in 1951 and went to work as his apprentice a year later.

D'Angelico's poor health, and the defection of his key luthier, Jimmy DiSerio, led him to close his business in 1959, only to be persuaded by a then-out-of-work D'Aquisto to start again, this time with D'Aquisto taking DiSerio's place. D'Angelico's death in 1962 left D'Aquisto to finish the last ten

guitars. It was the push D'Aquisto needed to open his own business making archtop guitars.

To say that D'Aquisto inherited his mentor's mantle is an understatement. D'Aquisto's archtop guitars are among the finest instruments ever made and include this 1988 acoustic archtop, the Avant Garde. D'Aquisto turned away from the traditional, Italianate motifs of guitar making, creating designs that were completely in tune with the modernist times in which he lived and worked. D'Aquisto, for example, abandoned the traditional f-holes —a staple of lutherie from the time of Stradivari— and replaced them with soft-edged lozenge shapes of varying sizes, sometimes two holes, sometimes four. And his sense of line, his shape making, was exquisite. Where D'Angelico had favored ornately shaped "broken scroll" headstocks, D'Aquisto's headstock designs became almost minimal, with a unique attention to line and form, and sometimes cut away to create a sense of lightness. Likewise, the tailpieces, once stamped metal, now became carved ebony, as were the pickguards, which became sleek, modernist expressions of D'Aquisto's shape-making line.

D'Aquisto died in 1995 at the age of fifty-nine, having made only 370 guitars. His legacy, however, has grown since his death, and appreciation for his stunning work has only deepened with time.

Manzer
Pikasso
1990

Type and body: Multi-neck, forty-two-string acoustic guitar. Spruce top. Indian rosewood body.
Neck and Fingerboard: Three mahogany necks. Three ebony fingerboards.
Pickups: One piezo electronic pickup.

The harp guitar is an ancient instrument, whether in the form of a lyre in ancient Greece or its superior cousin, the kithara, a professional version of the lyre, which apparently gave rise to the word *guitar*. Harp guitars have evolved from the lyre and the kithara and are an important subset of guitar making. Gibson's harp guitar, the Style U, was in production from 1902 until 1925, and was the most expensive instrument in the Gibson catalog of the time. Robbie Robertson plays a Gibson Style U in the Band's concert *The Last Waltz*. Far from being a freak instrument, the harp guitar has a long, and auspicious, history, tightly woven into the story of the guitar itself.

Canadian luthier Linda Manzer began her career with inspiration from Joni Mitchell, whose playing of the autoharp was becoming famous. Manzer built a dulcimer from a kit, and, from that moment on, she became infatuated with the idea of making guitars. In 1974, barely twenty-two years of age, she took an internship with noted Canadian luthier Jean Larrivée, whose company was becoming one of the leading acoustic guitar makers in the

world. A decade later, Manzer went to New York City to learn about archtops from the master, Jimmy D'Aquisto.

From those early moments in her education, Manzer has gone on to make guitars of exquisite quality for some of the greatest players in the world, but it is her close association with Pat Metheny that led to the creation of this extraordinary harp guitar, the Pikasso.

In the early 1980s, when Manzer was just a young luthier, Metheny asked her to make a guitar with "as many strings as possible." Metheny wanted to explore the harmonics of unstopped, resonating strings. And he wanted to have groups of strings in different tunings and registers that he could access in one guitar. Manzer's solution was the Pikasso, completed in 1986 after two years and one thousand hours of work. The Pikasso has four necks and forty-two strings, which, when tuned to concert pitch, put the guitar under one thousand pounds of pressure.

With a mixture of woods—including Indian rosewood for the back and sides, a spruce top, mahogany necks, and ebony fingerboards—the Pikasso has two sound holes and a unique piezoelectronic pickup system, including a hexagonal pickup under the six-string section that can be fed into Metheny's Synclavier computer, allowing him to access any of his sampled sounds. To enable Metheny to see all the strings at his disposal, Manzer made the body in a wedge shape—thinner on the top, under the player's arm, and thicker on the bottom, on his knees. This wedge has become a signature of Manzer's guitar designs.

Look for a video of Metheny playing his Pikasso on "The Sound of Water" or on one of his best-known compositions, "Into the Dream."

The guitar pictured is the Pikasso II, 1995.

Yamaha PA1511MS 1990

Type and body: Single-cutaway electric guitar. Alder body.
Neck and Fingerboard: Maple neck. Maple fingerboard.
Pickups: Two single-coil pickups and one humbucker pickup.

When considering Yamaha's musical instrument heritage, it is worth remembering that the Yamaha logo is three crossed tuning forks. It was adopted in 1898 and signifies its deep connection to music of all kinds, and not just to fast motorcycles.

Yamaha started with organs, then pianos, but did not begin making guitars until 1942, and even then limited itself for many years to producing budget-priced nylon-string classical guitars of excellent quality. This continued with their steel-string acoustic guitars, which have been greatly undervalued through the years. Undervalued, perhaps, but they sell in large numbers, and their players invariably love them for the quality of the build, the sweetness of the tones, and their playability.

When Yamaha began making electric guitars in the mid-1960s, the quality was good from the start, and it became really good with the introduction of the SG2000, which was considered an equal to anything coming from Gibson or Fender. It was so good that Carlos Santana started playing an SG2000 and continued for several years.

Mike Stern is a leading American jazz guitarist who played with legendary New York jazz/rock band Blood, Sweat & Tears before focusing on his own music and jazz. Long a Telecaster player, Stern's loss of his Fender in a robbery led him to a custom Telecaster-style guitar made by fellow Bostonian, luthier Michael Aronson. Which, in turn, led to Yamaha asking Stern if they could build him a custom guitar based around his Aronson model.

Although it looks like a Telecaster, it is very much a custom guitar, and one that sounds different than the Fender. Like the Telecaster, it has a solid body and a maple neck and fingerboard. The controls lie on a single plate, again like the Tele. However, it is its sound that makes it especially suited to Stern's rock-inflected jazz playing. The three pickups, all Seymour Duncan, are designed, on the one hand, to give the player a smooth jazz tone and, on the other hand, a raucous rock sound, or a combination of both.

For a guitar of such great sustain, lively power, and smooth tone, it is still overshadowed by the more expensive Gibsons and Fenders, and as a result, it is relatively, and unfairly, undervalued by collectors and guitar aficionados.

Charvel Surfcaster 1991

Type and body: Double-cutaway, semi-hollow-body electric guitar. Mahogany body.
Neck and Fingerboard: Maple neck. Rosewood fingerboard.
Pickups: Two single-coil "lipstick" pickups.

Charvel was formed in 1974 by former Fender tech Wayne Charvel as a guitar-refurbishing and parts business. When Charvel employee Grover Jackson bought the business in the late 1970s, he focused instead on making custom "restorations" of classic Fender guitars, the so-called "Superstrats." These guitars immediately found favor among the metal players, including Eddie Van Halen and Randy Rhoads, for whom Jackson would design a series of custom guitars under his own Jackson name.

Jackson moved production to Asia for a period, and finally sold the brand in 1989 to the Japanese company IMC. It was during this latter time that the Surfcaster model appeared. A decidedly retro design, the Surfcaster, with a semi-hollow body, two lipstick pickups, and a Fender-style vibrato, found an immediate following for its bright, thin tone coming from the two small lipstick pickups.

From a design perspective, the various styling cues are culled from a variety of sources, including Fender, Rickenbacker, and Danelectro. Often these design mash-ups become mishaps, whose failure is more or less guaranteed. This is not so with the Surfcaster, where Fender, whose Jazzmaster is reflected in the body shape, and Rickenbacker, whose signature swoosh appears on the body, combine to make a genuinely interesting guitar, and one with a reputation that has grown steadily through the decades.

For Charvel, this was decidedly a high point before the brand was acquired by Fender in 2002.

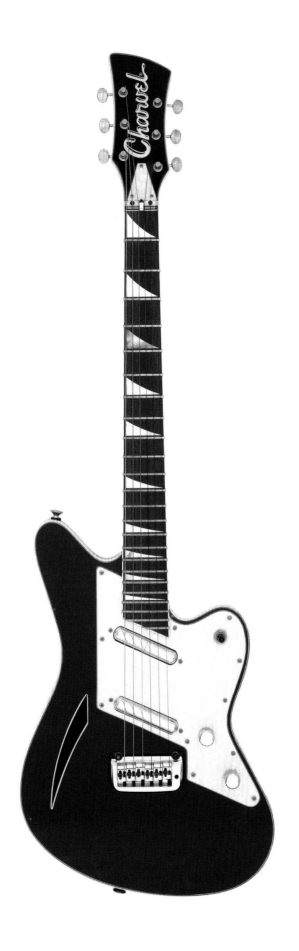

Robin
Machete
1991

Type and body: Solid-body electric guitar.
Laminated flame maple body.
Neck and Fingerboard: Rosewood neck.
Ebony fingerboard.
Pickups: Three humbucker pickups.

Robin is the guitar company founded by David Wintz in 1982. Wintz began by having his guitars made in Japan, before focusing production in Houston, where it remained for the next thirty years. Wintz shut down Robin Guitars in 2010, preferring to focus on electronics, including his signature pickups.

Wintz produced a number of interesting designs using high-end electronics and unusual Fender-based body shapes. Then in 1988 Wintz saw Def Leppard lead guitarist Phil Collen playing a Jackson special on MTV. Immediately struck by the connection between heavy metal and an unusual guitar design, Wintz went home and sketched the body of the Machete. Although he had no formal training in design, it took Wintz only thirty minutes to make the sketch, paying particular attention to the balance of the shape of the guitar. The balance is, indeed, there, with an elongated body shape reminiscent of both the Fender Jazzmaster and the Gibson Explorer, and most interesting of all, a signature split headstock. What is less obvious are the three horizontal steps on the upper and lower body, almost creating a pyramidal shape, with the uppermost plane holding the strings and pickups.

The body is flame maple, laminated to mahogany, with the neck running through the body, made of either rosewood or ebony, with three humbucker pickups. The characteristic split head comes from the reverse heads of earlier Robin models, which Wintz believed were easier for the guitarist to tune.

Jimi Hazel is a rocking Bronx guitarist whose afro-funk-metal band 24-7 Spyz has drawn comparisons to the Ramones, Jane's Addiction, and Red Hot Chili Peppers. Hazel is a learned and loquacious historian of the blues and rock, and he plays Robin guitars, including a vintage Machete. Look for Hazel's fiery guitar playing on "Break the Chains" by 24-7 Spyz.

Parker
The Fly
1997

Type and body: Solid-body electric guitar.
Carbon-fiber body laminated on wood core.
Vibrato tailpiece.
Neck and Fingerboard: Carbon-fiber composite
neck. Carbon-fiber composite fingerboard.
Pickups: Two humbucker pickups and Fishman
piezo electronic bridge pickup.

Joni Mitchell's oeuvre has been the subject of a comprehensive reevaluation in recent years, not least because of a wider understanding of her virtuoso guitar playing, her harmonic melody lines, and her subtle, open-tuning chord voicings, so different in effect from traditionally tuned chords. Indeed, her ability as a lyricist of abstract brilliance has also been reconsidered, leading to a general belief that Mitchell is one of the greatest singer/songwriters, guitarists, and performers of the late twentieth century.

Among her innovative approach to the guitar has been her choice of instruments. Looking for lightness, playability, and tone, Mitchell first chose the Ibanez George Benson, a light small-body guitar originally designed for George Benson's desire to have a guitar that was less prone to the feedback that bedeviled the large Gibson ES guitars favored by most jazz players.

Continuing that theme of lightness, quality, and tone, Mitchell then chose the Parker Fly, a new guitar designed in 1993 by luthier Ken Parker

in collaboration with electronics wizard Larry Fishman. Parker's design impulse was to make the lightest guitar he could, using composite materials consistent with new, contemporary electronics designed by Larry Fishman. Using a combination of wood and resin-plastic composites, Parker's guitar weighed in at less than five pounds (2.26 kg). The innovations continued with the unusual combination of traditional humbucker pickups with Fishman's piezo electronic bridge pickup, which used the changing pressure of the vibrating strings to create an electronic signal that closely resembled the tones of an acoustic guitar. This gave the player the ability to switch between an electric and acoustic sound in the same guitar, or a combination of both, features that would also be taken up by Paul Reed Smith for some PRS models. Parker's own vibrato tailpiece was a small engineering marvel that even on its own would have been a defining mark of a great guitar.

Parker's new design delivered an extraordinary and entirely fresh approach to the traditional solid-body guitar shape, which had been dominated by the shape of Fenders and Gibsons for several decades. Parker's body had a swooping German carve on the top of the body, an extended lower body with enough room for six switches, and two angular "horns" that framed the twin cutaways. Musicians loved the Parker Fly so much that Parker eventually sold his company, with all its patents, and returned to making top-quality archtop guitars.

Mitchell used her Parker Fly on her album *Taming the Tiger*, which she released to critical acclaim in 1998.

Dana Bourgeois
Martin Simpson
1998

Type and body: Single-cutaway acoustic guitar. Spruce top. Mahogany back and sides.
Neck and Fingerboard: Maple neck. Ebony fingerboard.

The search for more volume in an acoustic guitar has driven guitar design since the earliest days, and the large, jumbo, or Dreadnought size evolved to give the maximum volume in an acoustic instrument consistent with good tonal range and playability. Having satisfied that need, luthiers across the world have turned back to smaller guitars, ones where beauty of tone is paramount, because volume can largely be handled by pickups, microphones, and PA systems.

Dana Bourgeois is one of the best contemporary makers of steel-string acoustic guitars, and although he makes large Dreadnought instruments, it is his smaller guitars that have become among his most desirable.

Always interested in country music and bluegrass, Dana Bourgeois would show his guitars to bluegrass legend Tony Rice whenever Rice happened to be playing nearby. And it was Rice who preferred the sound of the smaller guitars that Bourgeois showed him, encouraging him to "put it in a bigger package."

From his factory in Lewiston, Maine, Bourgeois produces upward of four hundred guitars a year. Using traditional tone woods, including locally sourced Maine spruce, Bourgeois cures his woods in a heat process called torrefaction, which removes moisture quickly, hardening the woods in the process. Bourgeois often says he has been lucky that he got in at the beginning of a boom in handmade acoustic guitars. Perhaps, but if luck is a marriage of preparedness and opportunity, then Dana Bourgeois has been well prepared.

Dan Tyminski, a member of Alison Krauss's band Union Station, is not just one of the great bluegrass guitar virtuosos; he is also famous for being George Clooney's voice on "Man of Constant Sorrow," from the Joel and Ethan Coen movie *O Brother, Where Art Thou?* (2000). Tyminski plays a Bourgeois guitar, one of several in his collection.

The English guitarist and singer Martin Simpson wanted a large-sounding guitar, but he liked the twelve-fret smaller guitars that Bourgeois made. With his style of playing, Simpson needed access to fourteen or more frets. Bourgeois's solution, unusual for his guitars, was this shallow, elegant, sharp Florentine cutaway, the shape of which is echoed in the "snakehead" headstock. This combination of short scale and large lower body results in a guitar of extraordinary line and shape, coupled with a big, focused tone across each of the strings.

John Monteleone Radio Flyer 1998

Type and body: Archtop acoustic guitar. Spruce top. Maple back and sides.
Neck and Fingerboard: Maple neck. Ebony fingerboard.

The story of Italian immigrant luthiers building an American guitar industry is only now being fully explored. It is fair to say that without the finesse, skills, and deep understanding of these first- and second-generation Italian craftsmen, guitar brands, including Stella and National, might never have found success. The greatest of them became their own brands: John D'Angelico was the most sought-after archtop maker of his day. Jimmy D'Aquisto apprenticed with D'Angelico and took archtop guitars to a higher level of excellence. D'Aquisto was generally considered to be the greatest luthier of the twentieth century.

In the twenty-first century, one man has taken the lineage of D'Angelico and D'Aquisto and gone further. John Monteleone makes some of the most treasured guitars the world has seen, and they are the envy of players and collectors alike. Among those are the Four Seasons, a suite of four guitars, each different, each representing a season, inspired by Antonio Vivaldi's famous suite of violin concertos of the same name. And to take the inspiration a step further, John Monteleone himself commissioned a music piece for the guitars, composed by jazz guitarist Anthony Wilson. Called *Seasons: A Song Cycle for Guitar Quartet*, the suite explores each of the instruments and highlights the difference, in sound as well as in shape, of each of the guitars.

The Four Seasons guitars are stunningly beautiful in shape and sound. One of them, Summer, has a mandolin-style scroll on the body, reminiscent of the scroll on Orville Gibson's Style O guitar but also reminiscent of violin design in the great tradition of Italian lutherie. The guitars also have discrete sound holes set into the tops, a design innovation seen only by the guitarists themselves. These extra sound holes are to enable the guitarist to hear the same sound that emerges from the guitar's front.

Another guitar by Monteleone is the Radio Flyer. This remarkable guitar is a stunningly simple design, made with a carved spruce top, with a single, elegant, Venetian cutaway and sound holes that resemble the abstract shape of a dolphin as it leaps from the water. Monteleone has said that he named this guitar as a paean to the radio and his love of listening to it when he was a young boy. Radio Flyer is equally evocative of the little red wagon beloved of little boys and girls all over the United States.

Anthony Wilson is one of the most celebrated guitarist/composers in the world, and he plays a 1995 Radio Flyer. Among Wilson's large body of work, look for his 2016 album *Songs and Photographs* or his brilliant playing with singer Diana Krall, a highlight of which is Krall's 2002 album, *Live in Paris*.

Michael Lowe Lute 2001

Type and body: Venere-style bowl lute. European Spruce soundboard. Figured maple back.
Neck and Fingerboard: Sitka spruce neck with ebony veneer. Ebony fingerboard.

The story of the guitar goes back at least to the Greeks and the lyre, and beyond to the various plucked and strummed instruments of Africa, the Middle East, Asia, and Europe. The oud is the great fretless guitar of the Middle East, whose French name, *l'oud*, gives rise to the lute, that guitarlike instrument so beloved by Shakespeare. The oud, indeed, gives its name to the building of stringed musical instruments: lutherie.

As an instrument, the lute is commonly understood to be a large, multistringed instrument with a flat top and a large bowled back made of laths or ribs of hardwood, braced for strength. The top is usually made of spruce and features a latticework sound hole or "rose," usually carved from the top itself, and often of great and intricate beauty.

The lute is a staple of late renaissance and baroque music, where it is typically seen as an accompanying instrument, a "continuo" improvised by the player and strummed underneath the main melodic lines. The lute can have different tunings, different numbers of strings and courses, some stopped in the upper scales and others, the bass strings, allowed to resonate or be played according to the desires of the player.

With the tremendous revival of early music in the mid- to late twentieth century, led by the original instrument movement, in which the works of the great early music composers, from Telemann to Vivaldi, from Handel to Bach, were played on instruments of the time, and in a style appropriate to those instruments, the lute has seen a parallel revival. Championed by English guitarist Julian Bream, the lute's repertoire began to appeal to musicians for whom the classical guitar repertoire seemed limited. One such musician is English lutenist and educator Elizabeth Kenny, perhaps the most brilliant virtuoso of her time. Kenny's lute was commissioned from master luthier Michael Lowe. It took almost ten years for Lowe to create exactly the right lute for Kenny, and it was finally delivered in 2001.

A ten-course lute based on a design by the great Bolognese luthier Venere, this masterpiece is a perfect example of a Michael Rowe lute. Listen for Elizabeth Kenny's virtuoso playing on the 2004 recording of Vivaldi's *The Four Seasons* along with the wonderful Dutch violinist Janine Jansen.

Elizabeth Kenny playing her Michael Lowe lute after waiting a decade for it to be built.

PRS Custom Hollow-Body 2012

Type and body: Double-cutaway, hollow-body electric guitar. Mahogany body. CNC-milled spruce top and bottom.
Neck and Fingerboard: Mahogany neck. Ebony fingerboard.
Pickups: Two PRS 57/08 Low Turn pickups with Baggs/PRS piezo bridge pickup system.

Paul Reed Smith started his guitar company in 1985, but his story goes further back to his days in college, where, as part of his mathematics class, he made a guitar. But not just any guitar; Smith made a very good version of a Les Paul Junior, a model that became something of a benchmark obsession for Smith—in its quality, in its shape and form, and in the beauty of its tone.

Early fans included Peter Frampton and Carlos Santana, not only two of the greatest guitar virtuosos of the late twentieth century but true guitar aficionados. From that point onward, it was an upward trajectory for Smith and his designs, an ascent that continues four decades later.

Smith is devoted to the German carve, the effect of carving the outside of the guitar body so that the center of the body is higher than the edge. Another delightful design nuance is the dimples in which the tone and volume controls and the switches are located. The necks became famous for having inlaid dragons, then birds in flight, including eagles, which also adorned some headstocks, then, in a nod back to classical guitars, small ivory dots. But they weren't just dots; they were tiny moons in different phases.

Dublin-born guitarist Gerry Leonard has been a fixture on the New York music scene for several decades, becoming famous for playing with both David Bowie and Suzanne Vega, among many others. Leonard turned to Smith to make a special guitar, one that would function both as a straightforward rock electric but also as a folk-style acoustic guitar. Smith built a semi-hollow-body guitar that is both beautiful to look at and to play. Smith handles the electric guitar quality in the usual way, with two humbucker pickups of his own design. To get the best acoustic sound from the semi-hollow body, the bridge has individual piezo-electric sensors under each string. They work by converting the different pressures of the vibrating strings into electronic signals, which are then fed to a separate electronic circuit that can be fed into the guitarist's amp.

Leonard playfully uses the nickname Spooky Ghost for both his playing and his guitars, and in typical style, Smith made an inlaid white ghost on the headstock of Leonard's guitar, with custom "moon" fret markers on the fingerboard. Classically trained, Leonard's subtly virtuoso guitar playing has, in his harmonic shifts and chord voicings, all the hallmarks of the "sonic landscape" school of modern electric guitar players, which includes fellow Dubliner the Edge and Johnny Marr of the Smiths. Listen for Leonard's haunting arrangement of Bowie's "Loving the Alien," which made its debut when Bowie, backed only by Leonard, played a charity concert at New York's Carnegie Hall. From then on, Bowie preferred Leonard's arrangement, which he said was how he thought the song should always have sounded.

Michihiro Matsuda
#99
2015

Type and body: Deconstruction series guitar. Double-layer spruce, balsa, and Nomex honeycomb soundboard. Unique structural members provide rigidity to the body.
Neck and Fingerboard: Tempered maple neck. Ebony fingerboard with fan frets.
Pickups: One magnetic neck pickup. One piezo bridge pickup.

In the modern era of lutherie, almost anything is possible. Not just because it is now easier than ever to get a guitar to make a pleasing sound, but in this postmodern world, designers have allowed their imaginations to take them in hitherto unheard of directions to shape making of pure abstraction and joy.

Michihiro Matsuda was born in Japan and studied Japanese carpentry before moving to the United States to make guitars. Matsuda's workmanship is as extraordinary as his designer's imagination, with a precision and attention to detail that seem as if they are from another world.

This 2015 guitar is in what Matsuda refers to as his "deconstruction" style. His approach to this guitar is to deconstruct the player's preconceived notions about how a guitar should look and sound. Therefore, a player approaching, say, a Fender Telecaster knows from the shape that it is, in fact, a Tele, and further knows what it will feel like to pick it up and how it will play and sound.

The first thing to notice about Matsuda's design is the ebony fingerboard—not for the ebony but for the frets themselves, which are arranged as if in a fan. For the guitar to remain in tune, arranging the frets as a fan requires perfect fabrication of the neck, the frets themselves, the bridge saddle, and the tailpiece.

The materials Matsuda uses in this guitar are like a compendium of the best tone woods and hardwoods in the luthier's studio. The centerpiece body is of a double-top construction, with a spruce face and a balsa back, held together with Nomex honeycomb. The neck and frame around the top are made from figured maple using the Japanese technique of tempering, or roasting, the wood. The structural beams around the center of the guitar are of carved mahogany and wenge, with a back plate and leg rest of cedar. Both the fingerboard and bridge are made of ebony, and there is a pickguard of Matsuda's own mosaic style. The guitar has two pickups, a Kent Armstrong pickup in the neck as well as a Dazzo piezo electronic pickup under the top.

Flip Scipio Vega 2015

Type and body: Hollow-body guitar. Sitka spruce top. European maple back and sides.
Neck and Fingerboard: Quick-detach mahogany neck. Ebony fingerboard.
Pickups: One modified DeArmond 1100 pickup.

Brooklyn-based luthier Flip Scipio has made a great reputation as the go-to builder and repairman for guitar players all over the United States. Scipio was introduced to Boston jazz guitarist Mary Halvorson, who had a problem that she thought Scipio could solve. Halvorson's favorite guitar was her early 1970s Guild Artist Award, one of the great jazz guitars. Big and imposing, the Guild is difficult to travel with. Halvorson ran up against airline policies that increasingly prevented her from taking her precious Guild with her. She dreaded having to put the guitar in checked baggage. Halvorson needed a guitar that would not only sound great, as good as her venerable Guild, but one that she could dismantle, pack in a custom roll-aboard case, and bring with her as her carry-on luggage.

Scipio knew Halvorson's Guild well, and most important, he knew the neck dimensions, critically important to Halvorson's playing style. Scipio also owned a vintage DeArmond Rhythm Chief 1000 pickup, the classic jazz pickup of the 1960s, as installed on Halvorson's guitar. With these two starting points, Scipio's solution was to create a guitar with a detachable neck that would allow Halvorson to remove and reinstall the neck quickly and easily, with the strings remaining in place, when she needed to practice or play a gig. With a titanium mechanism fabricated in the Netherlands—coincidentally Scipio's birthplace—he set about making a large, jazzy flattop guitar with the best tone woods, the best electronics, and a detachable neck.

The result was the Vega, delivered to Halvorson's delight in 2015. The guitar itself is a thing of great beauty, both in its shape and in its sound. Archtops suffer terribly from feedback, and Scipio's solution to this problem was to create a removable soundpost that connected the back to the top of the guitar, obviating the feedback problem, and was accessible through a hole in the top side of the guitar. The guitar is not a carved archtop, but the flattop has a slight bow, thanks to the curved braces that Scipio designed to reinforce the thin spruce top. The rest of the guitar follows the path of her great vintage Guild: European maple back and sides, Sitka spruce top, mahogany neck, with an ebony fingerboard.

Scipio is a modernist in the European tradition and eschews unnecessary frills. Halvorson wanted inlays on the fingerboard, and he relented, creating beautiful mother-of-pearl and abalone abstract figures along the fingerboard that, in Scipio's mind, represent Mary Halvorson's music flowing from the guitar. To listen to Halvorson's avant-garde jazz, with its wonderful harmonic flow, chord progressions, and virtuoso fingering, listen to the 2018 albums *Ours* and *Theirs* with her band Thumbscrew.

Flip Scipio has made more straightforward guitars for many well-known players, including an electric high-strung guitar for Paul Simon, which is featured on Simon's 2000 album *You're The One* and an *archilaud*, or archlute, for Jackson Browne.

Greg Smallman & Sons Classical 2016

Type and body: Concert classical guitar. Lattice-braced western red cedar top or table. Madagascar rosewood back and sides.
Neck and Fingerboard: Durian (*Durio carinatus*) neck. Carbon-fiber fingerboard.

The workshop of Greg Smallman, in Esperance, in western Australia, is the center of much of the innovation and brilliance in modern classical guitar making. The correct name of the business is Greg Smallman Guitars & Sons Damon & Kym, and this is a family business, one with an ambition to match its reputation.

Steel-string acoustic guitars are often amplified, either within the guitars themselves or through some audio augmentation, which might include a mic, an amp, speakers, PA, or combinations of all. However, classical guitar repertoire, for the most part, demands that the guitars remain unamplified. This presents a challenge for luthiers, because players and audiences demand louder instruments that can be heard in bigger venues without losing the essence of why the classical guitar is so loved: its sweet, delicate tone; its power, when needed; and its sustain, where notes can hang in the air for the longest time.

Smallman began making guitars in 1972, initially in the style of the great twentieth-century Catalan luthier Ignacio Fleta, working with with traditional tone woods, spruce and cedar. Gradually, Smallman began experimenting with how the table, or top of the guitar, could be made thinner to let the sound emerge from and through the wood rather than purely through the sound hole. Abandoning the Spanish fan brace and other traditional bracing styles, Smallman developed a lattice of wood, and later composites, that gave the ultrathin top its rigidity. As if to offset the thinness of the tops, Smallman developed thicker carved backs for his guitars, a unique departure, using a violin or cello technique. The carved rest on the upper body of a Smallman guitar is not simply to protect the guitar's edge but is itself a structural member, connected through the sides to the back.

Early in his career, Smallman met guitar virtuoso and fellow Australian John Williams, and the two began a decades-long collaboration during which Williams's expert analysis of a guitar's sound spurred Smallman, now joined by his sons, to further develop the sound of his concert guitars.

Williams has used two Smallman guitars since 2000, both for his concerts and recordings. His 2018 Smallman guitar has a top of lattice-braced western red cedar, with back and sides of Madagascar rosewood. It was made with input from Williams on every aspect of the build and can be heard on Williams's 2019 recording *Vivaldi, Etc.!*

Among the other guitarists using Smallman guitars are Rupert Boyd in New York and the French guitarist Ingrid Riollot, who first fell in love with Smallman guitars, then fell in love with Damon Smallman, deepening an international family business of making and playing guitars.

Millimetric Instruments
MGS2
2016

Type and body: Single-cutaway, solid-body electric guitar. Various body woods, including ash, walnut, and maple. Painted finish.
Neck and Fingerboard: Aluminum neck. Maple fingerboard.
Pickups: Two proprietary single-coil pickups, inspired by the Travis Bean 500 pickups.

Florian Bouyou is a French luthier working in Montreal, Canada, making some of the most beautiful electric guitars ever seen. Born in Brittany, in western France, Bouyou started his musical life as a drummer, with a parallel artistic life as a graffiti artist and graphic designer. Dismantling guitars as a young man led him to Paris, where he learned about electric guitars by taking them apart and experimenting with different electronics, pickups, and amps—all the things young guitar fans do.

Needing to get serious about a career in guitars, Bouyou applied to the famous Bruand school of lutherie in Montreal, only to be turned down. Whereupon he pivoted and went to the cabinet-making school instead, where he became drawn into the world of midcentury-modern Scandinavian furniture, an influence that can be seen both in his shape making and color palettes today.

Millimetric Instruments, Bouyou's brand, started in 2012 with just one design, a minimal take on the oddly shaped Fender Jazzmaster, which was a big influence on Bouyou.

This guitar, the MGS2, is actually Bouyou's third production design. It has a deceptively simple, organic shape with a single cutaway and features two pickups of Bouyou's own design. The neck is aluminum, and in this, Bouyou has been influenced both by Travis Bean and also by the experimental U.S.-based design collective Obstructures. The guitar is designed to have custom flourishes according to the many choices in color and electronics available to the buyer, all within Bouyou's overall minimal, modernist design aesthetic. Everything is made in-house except for the Hipshot tuners.

Production output remains small, which is typical of such a high-quality handmade guitar. Given the success of Bouyou's designs, that is bound to change.

Ernie Ball Music Man St. Vincent Mass Education 2017

Type and body: Single-cutaway, solid-body electric guitar. Mahogany body with high-gloss polyester paint.
Neck and Fingerboard: Maple neck. Ebony fingerboard.
Pickups: Three DiMarzio mini-humbucker pickups.

For fifty years or more, the Ernie Ball Music Man company has been a wide-ranging music company with a deep legacy among professional guitar players, selling guitar-related products of all kinds, including its famous strings. The original Music Man business was founded in 1974 by ex-Fender employees and Leo Fender himself to make top-quality electric guitars and basses. Taken over in 1984 by Ernie Ball, and run today by the Ball family, Music Man continues to produce handmade electric guitars and basses of the highest quality.

Musician, singer, and songwriter Annie Clark, using the stage persona St. Vincent, has become recognized as one of the outstanding innovators of the electric guitar and a brilliant performer. Clark was closely involved in the design of her signature guitar, including the angular shape, which is forward-looking and modern. The shape, which might evoke an angular Fender Jazzmaster at first glance, but then doesn't, looks both original and contemporary, with vestiges of a double cutaway to give access to the guitar's twenty-two-fret fingerboard. The body is made of mahogany, while the neck is made of maple and the fingerboard is ebony, with inlaid fret markers designed by Clark.

The guitar has three DiMarzio mini-humbuckers with five-way switching and a custom vibrato, misnamed a tremolo, to give the player a lot of control over the guitar's sonic character.

Annie Clark's recorded output has received critical acclaim, both for her guitar playing brilliance and for the depth and breadth of her musicianship and songwriting. Clark's recorded output of seven albums includes her 2012 album *Love This Giant*, which is a collaboration with David Byrne. Listen for the sounds of her Ernie Ball Music Man guitar on her albums *MassEducation* (2018) and *Daddy's Home* (2021).

Rosenkrantz Pawtuxet 2017

Type and body: Steel-string acoustic guitar.
Cedar, bubinga, Nomex, honeycombs.
Neck and Fingerboard: Mahogany neck.
Rosewood fingerboard.

Rhode Island–based French architect, guitarist, and luthier Rachel Rosenkrantz is at the forefront of contemporary materials research, both as an academic specialism and as applied to the real challenges of making a guitar. Rosenkrantz spent a number of years working on building materials design and manufacture in architecture before realizing that she had many ambitions, among them to make guitars with new and different materials in new and different ways. Always at the service of sound, Rosenkrantz's guitars are working experiments in search of sonic beauty.

An active beekeeper, Rosenkrantz understands that bees have complex methods of visual and aural communication in their carefully organized colonies. Bees take orders from their leader, the queen, and each bee is part of a work group with specific duties. These orders are partly communicated through the acoustic properties of the honeycomb, which researchers have found can sustain sound signals over distances. Working with this theory, Rosenkrantz placed a piece of tone wood destined for a guitar's top inside a beehive, where the bees created a honeycomb structure directly onto the wood. After a full year inside the hive, the honeycomb structure was large enough to change locations from a beehive to a guitar.

Rosenkrantz placed the honeycomb (actually several parts of different honeycombs) into the guitar's body, allowing the vibrations generated by the guitar's strings to pass through the honeycomb and out into the ether to be enjoyed by the listener.

Such a bold experiment might be just a willful eccentricity if the guitar either looked awful or sounded terrible. The result is, however, the opposite; the guitar is a thing of extraordinary beauty and sounds wonderful, with soft, sustained middle and upper range and powerful bass notes.

The guitar is made of a combination of traditional tone woods, including cedar, bubinga, rosewood, and mahogany, with the honeycombs playing a significant structural role and finished with beeswax.

Rosenkrantz's guitars have attracted wide acclaim, not just for the experimental nature of the Pawtuxet (named for the Rhode Island river that runs past Rosenkrantz's studio in her adopted home in Rhode Island) but for her other designs, which include a violin and a classical guitar made in the style of Hauser.

Schorr Guitars
The Owl The Owl
2021

Type and body: Double-cutaway, hollow-body electric guitar. Sandwich-laminated maple top and back with open sides. Rosewood body.
Neck and Fingerboard: Apple and spruce neck. Bog oak fingerboard.
Pickups: Two single-coil pickups.

This is an exciting time for contemporary guitar-making, with innovative and forward-thinking designs coming from all parts of the world and very little of the devotion to Fender and Gibson that has, for four decades, dominated guitar shape making and construction.

Berlin-based Nicolai Schorr is both an artist and a luthier. Schorr began as an artist, focusing on painting and drawing during his art school days in Bremen, the shipbuilding city in the northwest of Germany. While still at school, Schorr had a side hustle buying broken guitars, fixing them, and selling them, presumably for a profit. This was how Schorr learned his trade, including skills in electronics and pickup design, talents that serve him well in his contemporary lutherie. After art school, and while playing in his band the Canoe Man, Schorr realized that his obsession with making guitars—*addicted* is the word he uses—had, in fact, become his profession.

The mysteriously named The Owl The Owl is a hollow-body guitar with a twenty-two-fret neck,

either six or seven strings (the seventh an extra bass string), a fixed bridge pickup, and a single sliding pickup. The sliding pickup is adjustable by moving it along a carbon-fiber rod so that it can be a neck pickup, a bridge pickup, or anything in between. The pickups are hand-wound by Schorr himself using an antique Singer sewing machine. Schorr uses the popular Hipshot tuners, from Stewmac in Athens, Ohio.

Schorr goes to great lengths with the shaping and finishing of every aspect of the guitar, ensuring a low footprint for each build, using chalk and natural mineral paints, applied by brush, to each guitar body. It is here that Schorr's training as an artist comes to the fore. The guitars are beautiful, and every detail is carefully considered, designed, and fabricated. This holds true down to the logo, of Schorr's own design, and the names he chooses for his designs, which he believes to be as much a part of the artistic process as the guitar itself.

Schorr built a partially fretless The Owl The Owl for Paris-based composer and singer Lionel Loueke, who is rapidly building a large international career as a jazz composer, educator, soloist, and recording artist. Loueke has worked with artists as diverse as Herbie Hancock, Norah Jones, and Angélique Kidjo, among many others. Look for Loueke's work on his 2020 streaming album, *HH*.

The guitar pictured is The Owl The Owl #041.

Taylor GTe Blacktop 2021

Type and body: Flattop acoustic guitar. Sitka spruce top. Walnut back and sides.
Neck and Fingerboard: Mahogany neck. Eucalyptus fingerboard.
Pickups: Built-in Taylor "behind the saddle" piezo electronic pickup sensors.

When Bob Taylor and his partner, Kurt Listug, formed Taylor Guitars in 1974 in a burst of enthusiasm, little did they know that half a century later Taylor would be a giant among guitar makers, would be employee owned, and would be making some of the best-sounding and most playable guitars ever made.

The beginnings were inauspicious. While still a teenager, Taylor was working in a hippie guitar store in San Diego when the owner decided to call it quits. Taylor and twenty-one-year-old Listug, more or less on a whim, scrambled to get the money together and bought the place. They wanted to sell, repair, and ultimately make guitars. That was then. Today, Taylor Guitars sells more than two hundred thousand guitars ever year, all of them of high quality.

The heart of Bob Taylor's vision for guitars is great sound and playability. As a luthier, one of Taylor's earliest innovations was to stabilize the neck, long a problem on acoustic guitars. Traditionally, the neck is glued to the body. The fingerboard is, of course, glued to the neck until, that is, the neck joins the body. After that, the neck is on its own, glued to the top of the guitar. The trouble with this setup is that the thin top is notoriously prone to changes in temperature and humidity, which causes it to move. And if the body moves, the part of the fingerboard that is attached to it moves, too.

Taylor's solution was a tightly engineered neck that bolts to a precise pocket in the body. The neck is micro-adjustable with shims, and the neck continues to the nineteenth fret, with the fingerboard attached.

Taylor was also eager to break away from the dominance of large sizes in guitar making, reasoning that children, young adults, people who have different-sized hands, and people with different desires needed comfortable guitars to play. His smallest guitar was known as the Baby Taylor, and they sold in the thousands.

A guitar's unique voice became the obsession when Andy Powers joined Taylor Guitars to take over guitar design and fabrication as chief luthier. A highly trained and fantastic guitarist in his own right, Powers had been building guitars since he was a young boy. He had it in his hands and his head. Powers addressed bracing to further enhance the stability of the guitar's tops as well as to create what all luthiers crave: sweet tones across all strings, with power and sustain.

One of Powers's newest designs is the compact Taylor GTe, with a Sitka spruce top and walnut back and sides. As well as being Taylor's smallest guitar, it is comfortable, playable, and has a beautiful sound. At a time when independent guitar builders are rethinking how guitars can sound, Powers's ability to think like an indie but put his desires as a musician and his skills as a luthier to the fore makes it a special time for American production guitars of the highest quality.

Cowbrand Design Mars Guppy: Irwin 2022

Type and body: Custom short-scale, semi-hollow-body parlor electric guitar. Cherry top. Select poplar chambered back.
Neck and Fingerboard: Laminated three-piece maple neck. Wenge fingerboard.
Pickups: Two hand-wound custom single-coil pickups. Fishman Triple Play complete wireless MIDI system.

Michael King brings a polymath's brilliance to everything he does, including graphic design, in which he has found separate fame; his encyclopedic knowledge of the history and popular culture of music, especially the blues; and his guitar playing, which brings him to gigs in and around his native St. Louis.

While still in high school, King started as a repairman of violins in a local music store. The store owner had a contract with the St. Louis schools to provide violins and other musical instruments, and these "loaners" often came back damaged. It was King's job to fix them, and he quickly became an expert in the finer points of violin repair. He moved on to guitars, and became both a perceptive historian and an expert repairman.

King's guitars, made under his company name, Cowbrand, look back to some of the design cues of midcentury Italian automotive design, and also to another obsession: vintage science fiction television, especially anything written by Irwin Allen. The subtleties of King's graphic design references are such that if you don't get the inside references, you won't miss them. What matters is the whole design and, in this, King is a master.

The Mars Guppy was made for guitarist Vernon Reid, whose band, Living Colour, has produced some of the most shape-shifting guitar music of the last several decades. An earlier collaboration with Bill Frisell, *Smash & Scatteration*, gave King a starting point for the electronics of the guitar, which feature a Fishman complete wireless MIDI setup. This to accommodate Reid's love of synthesized guitar voices.

The semi-hollow-body guitar has a short scale, a "chambered" body, and includes two of King's self-wound pickups. King often uses unusual woods, and in the past has used one-hundred-year-old pine and Douglas fir, reclaimed from local St. Louis demolition sites. For the Irwin, King used cherry for the top, which he painted with a water-base acrylic paint. The finish and graphics echo the *Lost in Space* sci-fi color theme and overall graphic aesthetic. With a see-through pickguard and simple, perfect knobs, the guitar exudes class and style. The maple neck is a specially requested carve, a vintage deep V-neck, the guitarist's preferred neck profile.

Glossary

Action The distance of the strings above the fingerboard, which affects the playability of the guitar.

Air guitar Performative, often exaggerated, playing of an imaginary guitar, usually electric, but can include classical and acoustic. See "Nut."

Alfabeto An early Italian form of guitar notation in which a harmonic chord was given a name.

Alnico An iron alloy containing varying quantities of aluminum (Al), nickel (Ni), cobalt (Co), and other metals. It is used for making permanent magnets and is a component of many guitar pickups.

Archtop A guitar in which the top and bottom of the guitar's body have been carved to form their shape, which is a gentle arch. The arch contributes to the structural integrity of the guitar body, reducing the reliance on internal bracing to provide stiffness.

Arpeggio A musical term describing a chord played as a sequence of individual notes instead of being strummed as a single harmonic sound.

Baile One of the three principal elements of flamenco, meaning "dance." The others being "Cante" and "Toque."

Binding The border or edge detail that is often inlaid into the guitar's body and often in the fingerboard. The binding effectively seals the edges of the guitar's body and sides. It can be a highly decorative design flourish.

Bookmatch Often used on guitar tops, a piece of thin wood that has been split into two pieces with joined edges that mirror each other. The visual effect is of an open book, hence, for example, "bookmatched spruce top."

Bout When viewed vertically, the upper bout is the section of the guitar body from the waist to the neck joint. The lower bout is the section from the waist to the tail. In this book, "upper body" and "lower body" have generally been used instead of "bout."

Braces Thin strips of wood glued to the inside of a guitar body to add stiffness and control vibration.

Bridge A device on the guitar that supports, and sometimes anchors, the strings on the body. In an acoustic guitar, the bridge transfers the sounds of the strings to the top of the guitar, which in turn causes the vibrations to move air in the chamber of the guitar. Combined with the nut, the bridge positions the strings at the correct height above the guitar fingerboard. In electric guitars, the bridge is sometimes adjustable for each string, enabling fine-tuning of the strings.

Cante One of the three principal elements of flamenco, meaning "song." The others being "Baile" and "Toque." See elsewhere in the glossary.

Capo A device with a plastic or rubber sheathed metal bar to clamp across the fingerboard to raise the pitch of the strings.

Chitarra battente A baroque Italian guitar that was strummed instead of being plucked. *Battente* is the Italian for "beaten," meaning strummed.

Course A course is a pair of strings, usually tuned in unison, sometimes in octaves. Modern 12-string guitars have six "courses."

Cutaway A space cut away from the guitar body near the neck to allow the guitarists' fingers to reach the upper frets of the fingerboard. Can be single or double cutaway. See also "Florentine" and "Venetian."

Dreadnought The largest body in typical acoustic guitars. The word was first used by Martin to describe its largest body type. Various types of Mexican guitars have bodies that are larger than the Dreadnought. See also "Jumbo."

Duende The ineffable spirit of flamenco music performance.

Electromagnetic pickup A type of pickup that uses a coil of copper wire wound around a magnet. When vibrations from the strings cause the magnet to vibrate, an alternating current is induced in the coil, which is then routed to an amplifier. See also "Pickup."

Fan bracing A series of thin wooden strips arrayed in a fan and glued to the underside of the guitar top to stiffen the top.

Fingerboard The part of the neck of a guitar containing the frets. Used synonymously with "Fretboard."

Florentine cutaway A cutaway with a sharp, pointed profile. See also "Cutaway."

Fret Thin strips of usually wire laid across the fingerboard. Notes on a string are changed by pressing the string between two frets. On Hawaiian and slide guitars, frets are simply visual aids, because the notes are changed by sliding a metal bar on the strings.

German carve Generally ascribed to Rickenbacker designer Roger Rossmeisl, the German carve is a filleted indent that is carved around the edge of a guitar body's top, and occasionally, its back.

Glissando More correctly portamento, a musical term describing the effect of gliding between two or more notes. Used on Hawaiian and other slide guitar playing.

Harmonic Touching a string lightly without pressing the string onto the fret. It has the effect of sounding some harmonic elements of a note and eliminating others. Heard most often in classical guitar playing and in jazz. Paul McCartney plays the final note of his Beatles song "Blackbird" as a harmonic chord.

Hawaiian guitar A style of guitar popularized in the early part of the twentieth century, in which the strings are raised off the fingerboard, which is usually fretless. The guitarist uses a steel bar or tube to change the pitch of the strings. See also "Resonator or resonating guitars."

Headstock The neck extension where the strings are usually both anchored and tuned by the tuning machines.

Heel The shaped block of wood supporting the joint between the guitar neck and body.

Humbucker, humbucking pickup A type of guitar pickup developed by Gibson with two copper-wire coils having opposing polarities that cancel the "hum" or feedback typical of single-coil pickups.

Luthier A guitar maker. Is also used to describe a maker of other stringed instruments, including violins, cellos, and lutes.

Mustache The decorative shape of early guitar bridges. Seen on baroque guitars and on some contemporary acoustic guitars.

Nut The bar that holds the strings in position at the correct height above the fingerboard, where the fingerboard joins the headstock. The term is also used to refer to a participant in an air-guitar competition.

PAF or P.A.F. Type of humbucker pickup developed by Seth Lover for Gibson and used between 1956 and 1962. Acronym for Patent Applied For.

Pickguard A plastic piece attached to the guitar body to protect it from damage from being struck by the pick or fingers. Often with expressive shape or colors.

Pickup Any type of device that converts nearby vibrations into an electrical signal that can be routed to an amplifier.

Piezoelectric pickup A type of guitar pickup that converts the physical stresses from vibrating strings into electrical signals that are routed to an amplifier.

Potentiometer ("Pot") Electric guitar tone and volume controls are potentiometers, which vary the electronic inputs from the guitar pickups before routing to the amplifier.

Portamento See "Glissando."

Purfling The border or edge detail that is inlaid into the guitar's body. Often used synonymously with "Binding."

Resonator or resonating guitar A steel-string guitar in which the sound of the strings is acoustically amplified through a metal cone, or cones, inserted into the body.

Rose or rosette The ornamented border surrounding the sound hole of an acoustic or classical Spanish guitar. Also the highly fretted decoration that fills the sound hole of lutes and baroque guitars.

Saddle A component of the bridge, usually a thin bar of plastic that anchors and supports the strings on the bridge.

Scale or scale length The length of the strings. In practice, the length of the neck and fingerboard, which is calculated as half of the overall string length.

Single-coil pickup A type of pickup using a magnet and a single coil of copper-wire coil. See also "Electromagnetic pickup."

Solid-body guitar A guitar without a resonating chamber, whose body is made of wood or other material.

Steel guitar, also pedal steel, lap steel A guitar in which the strings are positioned high above the fingerboard and played with a steel bar held in the hand and slid along the strings to select different notes while picked with the right hand. Original Hawaiian-style guitars, such as the Weissenborn, were played on the lap. Modern steel guitars are electric and sit on a special stand.

Struts See "Braces."

Sunburst A graduated lacquer finish on acoustic and electric guitars achieved by spraying dark lacquer over a light background.

Tablature or tab The musical notation that shows the player's fingers in position on the fingerboard and strings.

Table or soundboard The top of an acoustic guitar body.

Tailpiece A device used to anchor the strings, separate from the bridge.

Tone wood The wood used for the soundboard of an acoustic guitar.

Toque One of the three principal elements of flamenco, meaning "guitar

playing." The others being "Baile" and "Cante." See previously in the glossary.

Trapeze tailpiece A device used to anchor the strings, separate from the bridge. Most often seen on electric guitars, with a bar for the string ends, attached to the guitar with two metal rods that, in turn, are attached to the tail of the guitar.

Tremolo A rapid variation of the volume of a note. The term is often misused, as in "Tremolo Arm." See Vibrato Arm, below.

Truss rod A metal rod inserted into the neck of the guitar to strengthen the neck, lessening any tendency of the guitar neck to deform under the tensile load of the strings. Many truss rods are adjustable for the height of the strings above the fingerboard.

Tune-o-matic bridge An adjustable bridge developed by Gibson for its electric guitars.

Venetian cutaway A cutaway with a soft, radiused profile. See also "Cutaway."

Vibrato arm A device on electric guitars to alter the pitch of the strings, making it higher or lower. Also known as a "whammy bar" or "Bigsby," after its inventor, Paul Bigsby. Often mistakenly called a Tremolo Arm.

Vibrola Gibson version of the Bigsby style of vibrato arm.

Further Reading

Babluck, Andy. *The Story of Paul Bigsby: Father of the Modern Electric Guitar*. Milwaukee: Hal Leonard Books, 2009.

Bacon, Tony, and Scott Chinery. *The Chinery Collection: 150 Years of American Guitars*. London: Balafon Books, 1996.

Bacon, Tony, and Paul Day. *The Ultimate Guitar Book*. New York: Alfred A Knopf, 1991.

Ballestri, Marco. *Wandré, the Artist of Electric Guitar*. Modena, Italy: Anniversary Books, 2014.

Baños, Ignacio "Nacho." The Blackguard. Valencia, Spain: Manfredo Music SL, 2005.

Bellow, Alexander. *The Illustrated History of the Guitar*. Van Nuys, CA: Franco Colombo Publications, 1970.

Bellson, Julius. *The Gibson Story*. Kalamazoo, MI: Julius Bellson, 1973.

Bitoun, Julien. *Guitars & Heroes*. Richmond Hill, Canada: Firefly Books, 2018.

Bogdanovich, John S. *Classical Guitar Making*. New York: Sterling, 2007.

Burrows, Terry, et al. *1001 Guitars To Dream of Playing Before You Die*. London: Cassell Illustrated, 2013.

Carter, Walter. *Gibson Guitars: 100 Years of an American Icon*. Los Angeles: General Publishing Group, 1994.

David, George. *The Flamenco Guitar*. Madrid: The Society of Spanish Studies, 1966.

Dixon, Jamie, et al. *The World's Greatest Electric Guitars*. London: Carlton Books Limited, 2018.

Dobney, Jason Kerr. *Guitar Heroes: Legendary Craftsmen from Italy to New York*. New York: The Metropolitan Museum of Art, 2011.

Dobney, Jason Kerr, Craig Inciardi, et al. *Play It Loud: Instruments of Rock and Roll*. New York: The Metropolitan Museum of Art, 2019.

Evans, Tom and Mary Anne. *Guitars from the Renaissance to Rock*. New York: Paddington Press Ltd., 1977.

The Galpin Society Journal (www.galpinsociety.org/journal.htm). An indispensable resource for anyone interested in musical instruments.

Gruhn, George, and Walter Carter. *Acoustic Guitars and Other Fretted Instruments*. San Francisco: Miller Freeman, Inc., 1993.

Gruhn, George, and Walter Carter. *Electric Guitars and Basses, an Illustrated History*. San Francisco: Miller Freeman, Inc., 1994.

Gruhn, George, and Walter Carter. *Gruhn's Guide to Vintage Guitars*. San Francisco: Backbeat Books, 1999.

Guralnick, Peter. *Sweet Soul Music: Rhythm and Blues and the Southern Dream of Freedom*. New York: Harper and Row, 1986.

Guralnick, Peter. *Last Train to Memphis: The Rise of Elvis Presley*. Boston: Little, Brown & Co., 1994.

Guralnick, Peter. *Searching for Robert Johnson*. Boston: Little, Brown & Co., 2020.

Hunter, Dave. *Ultimate Star Guitars*. New York: Quarto Publishing Group, 2017.

Kelly, Martin, Terry Foster, and Paul Kelly. *Fender, the Golden Age, 1946–1970*. London: Cassell Illustrated, 2010.

Kelly, Martin, and Paul Kelly. *Rickenbacker Guitars: Out of the Frying Pan, into the Fireglo*. New York: Phantom Books, 2021.

Kuronen, Darcy. *Dangerous Curves*. Boston: MFA Publications, 2000.

The Metropolitan Museum of Art. *The Spanish Guitar*. New York: The Metropolitan Museum of Art, 1992.

Moust, Hans. *The Guild Guitar Book*. Milwaukee: Hal Leonard, 1999.

Osborne, Nigel, et al. *2,000 Guitars: The Ultimate Collection*. London: Outline Press, 2009.

Quiñones, Fernando. *El Flamenco, Vida y Muerte*. Madrid: Plaza y Canés, 1971.

Romanillos, José L. *Antonio de Torres, Guitar Maker*. Westport, CT: The Bold Strummer, 1987.

Schiller, David. *Guitar, the World's Most Seductive Instrument*. New York: Workman, 2019.

Shaw, Robert, Peter Szego, et al. *Inventing the American Guitar*. Milwaukee: Hal Leonard Books, 2013.

Smith, Richard R. *The Complete History of Rickenbacker Guitars*. Fullerton, CA: Centerstream Publishing, 1987.

Smith, Richard R. *Fender: The Sound Heard 'Round the World*. Fullerton, CA: Garfish Publishing Company, 1995.

Stratton, Stephen Samuel. *Nicolo Paganini: His Life and Work*. Wentworth Press, 2019.

Sudo, Philip Toshio. *Zen Guitar*. New York: Simon & Schuster, 1997.

Thiel-Cramer, Barbara. *Flamenco: The Art of Flamenco, Its History and Development Until Our Days*. Stockholm: Remark AB, 1991.

Trynka, Paul. *The Electric Guitar: An Illustrated History*. San Francisco: Chronicle Books, 1995.

Turnbull, Harvey. *The Guitar from the Renaissance to the Present Day*. London: BT Batsford Ltd., 1974.

Tyler, James. *The Early Guitar*. London: Oxford University Press, 1980.

Washburn, Jim, and Richard Johnson. *Martin Guitars, an Illustrated Celebration*. Emmaus, PA: Rodale Press, Inc., 1997.

Wheeler, Tom. *American Guitars: An Illustrated History*. New York: Harper Perennial, 1992.

Wright, Michael. *Guitar Stories Vol. 1: The Histories of Cool Guitars*. Bismarck, ND: Vintage Guitar Books, 1995.

Wright, Michael. *Guitar Stories Vol. 2: The Histories of Cool Guitars*. Bismarck, ND: Vintage Guitar Books, 2000.

Index

Picture Credits

Every reasonable effort has been made to acknowledge the ownership of copyright for photographs included in this volume. Any errors that may have occurred are inadvertent, and will be corrected in subsequent editions provided notification is sent in writing to the publisher.

p.24: Richard E. Aaron / Getty Images; p.75: Berenice Abbott / Getty Images; p.8 top left: AGE Fotostock; p.15 bottom: akg-images / Album / sfgp; p.47–49: akg-images / François Guénet; p.8 top right: akg-images / François Guénet; p.19: Robert Altman / Getty Images; p.155: Jorgen Angel / Getty Images; p.91: Photo courtesy of the Arhoolie Foundation; p.27 bottom: Artepics / Alamy Stock Photo; p.61, 77, 85–87, 109–111, 125, 133, 135, 149, 153: George Aslaender/ Retrofret Vintage Guitars p.247–249: Ultan Guilfoyle p.259: Ernie Ball Music Man; p.70–73: Photos by David Bean, courtesy of *The North American Guitar*; p.15 top: Stefano Bianchetti / Bridgeman Images; p.30, 31 bottom: Blank Archives / Getty Images; p.207: Bonhams; p.17 top, 27middle: Bridgeman Images; p.23: CBS Photo Archive / Getty Images; p.127: Photo © Christie's Images / Bridgeman Images; p.157: TomCopi / Getty Images; p.269: Cowbrand Design; p.205: CRAVE Guitars; p.39: De Agostini Picture Library / agefotostock; p.81, 107: Dorling Kindersley ltd / Alamy Stock Photo; Dorling Kindersley ltd / Alamy Stock Photo; p.97, 241–243: Dream Guitars – Logan Wells; p.8 bottom right, 161: Elderly Instruments; p.83: © Claude Germain / Philharmonie de Paris; p.163–165: Getty Images; p.33 top: Getty Images / Handout; p.197: Jeff Goode / Getty Images; p.34 bottom: Christie Goodwin/TAS / Contributor; p.63: Göteborgs Auktionsverk and Auctionet; p.137: *Guitar Magazine* Japan; p.177: *Guitarist Magazine* / Getty Images; p.231: *Guitarist Magazine* / Getty Images; p.99, 95, 115–117, 159, 168–169, 187, 199, 203, 217, 219, 233: Heritage Auctions, HA.com; p.27 top: Heritage Images / Getty Images; p.129: Heritage Images / Heritage Art / akg-images; p.28: Hoberman Publishing / Alamy Stock Photo; p.123: Jonathan Kirn / Alamy Stock Photo; p.105: Julien's Auctons/ Summer Evans; p.245: Elizabeth Kenny; p.201: Scott Legato / Getty Images; p.119–121: Leonard Auction, Inc.; p.79: Library of Congress Prints and Photographs Division Washington, D.C. 20540 USA; p.215: Lyle Lovett; p.181: Larry Marano / Getty Images; p.188: Mark and Colleen Hayward / Getty Images; p.51: © Alberto Martinez/Orfeo Magazine / Philharmonie de Paris; p.251: Matsuda Guitars; p.101: Image copyright The Metropolitan Museum of Art/Art Resource/Scala, Florence; p.225: Michael Ochs Archives / Getty Images; p.257: Millimetric instruments; p.7 top: Mondadori Portfolio / Getty Images; p.44: Courtesy of the Musical Instrument Museum, Phoenix, Arizona; p.113: Nigel Osbourne / Getty Images; p.7 bottom: © NPL – DeA Picture Library / G. Cigolini / Bridgeman Images; p.131, 171, 173, 179, 191, 193, 211, 227, 229, 235, 239: Nigel Osbourne / Getty Images; p.34 top: Peter Pakvis / Contributor; p.17 center: Pictorial Press Ltd / Alamy Stock Photo; p.31 top left: PictureLux / The Hollywood Archive / Alamy Stock Photo; p.24 bottom: Christopher Polk/Shutterstock; p.22 top: Popperfoto / Getty Images; p.32: Michael Putland / Getty Images; p.20: Radio Times / Getty Images; p.143: Frédéric Ragot / Getty Images; p.139: David Redfern / Getty Images; p.151: Ebet Roberts / Getty Images; p.261–263: Courtesy of Rachel Rosenkrantz; p.55, 56–57, 59, 67, 69: Photos by Felix Salazar, courtesy of Guitar Salon International; p.28 top: © 2022. Photo Scala, Florence; p.22 bottom: Max Scheler – K & K / Getty Images; p.265: Nicolai Schorr; p.253: Flip Scipio; p.31: top right: Shawshots / Alamy Stock Photo; p.89, 223, 225: Courtesy of Siccas Guitars; p.33 bottom: sjvinyl / Alamy Stock Photo; p.213, 237: Division of Cultural and Community Life, National Museum of American History, Smithsonian Institution; p.93: Jeromie B Stephens; p.209: Pete Still / Getty Images; p.267: Taylor Guitars; p.103: The Acoustic Room; p.12 bottom: Jacques Torregano / akg-images; p.8, 145–147: Truetone Music, Santa Monica, Ca. / Ry Cooder; p.17 bottom, 167, 168–169: *TV Times* / Getty Images; p.175: Darwin Webb; p.40–43, 53, 65: Jake Wildwood; p.141: Witherell's Inc.

Acknowledgments

I could not have written this book without the generosity and friendship of singer, songwriter, and actor **Lyle Lovett**. Lyle took time off in the middle of a concert tour to photograph his Collings #29, which he generously allowed me to feature.

Flip Scipio is a Brooklyn-based luthier who builds and restores guitars and related fretted instruments for some of the world's best players. Flip has guided my hand from the very beginning of this book with erudition, humor, and expertise.

These two friends were my informal board of advisors, and I am in their debt.

St. Louis guitarist, luthier, graphic designer, and historian **Michael King** is not only a great guitar maker; he is a polymath on the history of the American guitar and guitar music. Michael's gentle corrections on my understanding of the blues were timely.

With great humor and expertise, Texas writer **Tim Madigan** educated and corrected me on the enduring boomer romance of the guitar solo, most notably Dave Gilmore's paean to muscle relaxants and Anglo-rock malaise, "Comfortably Numb."

Composer, guitarist, and educator **James Moore** was once my guitar teacher. Now he is my guide to the world of contemporary classical guitar repertoire.

My friend and collaborator Professor **Charles Falco** enlightened me on the mysteries of magnetism, electricity, and guitar pickups, among many other things.

English luthier and scholar **Gary Southwell** taught me the historical greatness of Luis Panormo's classical guitars.

Lutenist **Elizabeth Kenny** opened my ears to the wonders of the baroque repertoire for the guitar and the lute, and how it should be played.

I am also grateful to a number of other people for many helpful discussions and insights on guitars and guitar music, including:

Fiona Maddocks
G. Marq Roswell
Steve McCreary
Angela Thomas
John Monteleone
John Williams
Dana Bourgeois
Bob Geldof
Gerry Leonard
Paul Harrington
Chris Franklin
Anne Rapp
Emilia Terragni
Mitzi Pratt
Rachel Rosenkrantz
Catherine Owens
Dana DiPrima
Stephanie Carendi
Martin Smith
Bill Megalos
Tom O'Brien
Sean Eden
Peter Finlay
Will Gatti
Chris Aggs
Roger Sherman
Jared Zaugg
Rupert Boyd
Valerie Lasser
Greg Jordan
Tom Efinger
Justin Fair
Edwin Chan
Michelle Kaufmann
Karen Stein
George Tiffin
Cathrine Ellis
Jennifer Rogers
Judith Cox
Clare Churly
Sarah Bell
Emma Barton
Dianne Hurley
Alanna Guilfoyle
Tomaso Rock
Sofia Rock

About the Author

Ultan Guilfoyle is a film producer, director, curator, and writer whose films have appeared on HBO, Bravo, and PBS in the United States, and the BBC and Channel 4 in Britain. While at the BBC, he produced music and arts programs, including *The Whistle Test* and *Live Aid*. In 2001 he produced the film *1071 Fifth Avenue* for ITV's *The South Bank Show* with creative partner Bob Geldof. Working with the late director Sydney Pollack, Guilfoyle's film *Sketches of Frank Gehry* was an Official Selection of the Cannes Film Festival and was released theatrically by Sony Pictures Classics. Guilfoyle has made films with architects Renzo Piano, Annabelle Selldorf, and Japanese Pritzker Prize winning firm SANAA, as well as Frank Gehry, with whom he has worked for more than twenty-five years. Guilfoyle was the founding director of the Film Department at the Solomon R. Guggenheim Museum in New York, where he later cocurated the landmark exhibition *The Art of the Motorcycle*. In 2021 Guilfoyle cocurated the exhibition *The Motorcycle: Design, Art, Desire* for QAGOMA in Brisbane, Australia. His writing has appeared in international publications including the *New York Times*, the *Independent*, and *Design* magazine. This is Guilfoyle's fourth book for Phaidon Press.

Phaidon Press Limited
2 Cooperage Yard
London E15 2QR

Phaidon Press Inc.
65 Bleecker Street
New York, NY 10012

phaidon.com

First published 2023
© 2023 Phaidon Press Limited

ISBN 978 1 83866 558 6

A CIP catalogue record for this book is available from the
British Library and the Library of Congress.

Commissioning Editor: Emilia Terragni
Project Editor: Tom Furness and Clare Churly
Production Controller: Gif Jittiwutikarn
Design: Phaidon Press Limited

Printed in China

The publisher would like to extend special thanks to Theresa
Bebbington, Sarah Bell, Hilary Bird, Rich Cochrane, Josh Lee,
Jon Levy, Laine Morreau, Sean McGeady, João Mota, Michele
Robecchi, Mat Smith, and Tracey Smith for their contributions
to the book.